PUNK PIONEERS

JENNY LENS

Foreword by Glen E. Friedman

UNIVERSE

First published in 2008 in the United States of America by
Universe Publishing
A Division of Rizzoli International Publications, Inc.
300 Park Avenue South
New York, NY 10010
www.rizzoliusa.com

Designed by Mark A. Martinez
Typesetting by Tina Henderson

2008 2009 2010 2011 / 10 9 8 7 6 5 4 3 2 1

ISBN-10: 0-7893-1589-0
ISBN-13: 978-0-7893-1589-2
Library of Congress Catalog Number: 2007905841

Printed in China

This book owes its birth to Glen E. Friedman for his persistent and skillful presentation to
Rizzoli/Universe, to my patient and calm editor, Jacob Lehman (thank you!), and to Mark A.
Martinez, my best friend from punk, my soul brother, who knows my archive as well and in some
cases better than I, and who designed my first solo book. Mark took my breath away with his
skillful interpretation of my rough layouts. Years ago I begged, cajoled, and encouraged him to
become a designer because he's the most creative and fun person I shall ever know. Gratitude to
Rizzoli for hiring him and allowing my input. Creating this book saved my life and gave me a
reason to continue in a time of utter despair, disappointment, and pain.
    Thanks to my long-time pals archivist/musician David Owen Jones, Michael Pilmer,
Rosemarie Patronette, Alice Bag and her family, Brian Grillo, Michael Wilcox, Patrick O'Leary,
Kurt Porter, Dr. Don Trepany, Brad Elterman, Gail Zone, Raymond Leon Roker, Linda Ramone,
Mandy Stein and her parents Seymour and Linda (RIP), Danny Fields, Mickey Leigh, Roger
Gastman, Shepard Fairey, Adam Starr and Todd Nakamine at UMG, Marina del Rey and Genny
Body (Backstage Pass, unfortunately omitted from this book, but in the next one!), Michelle
Habell-Pallan, Holly George-Warren, and everyone who ever emailed me, stopped me at a party or
art show and told me how much my photos mean, who picked up a camera, a record, a CD, a
guitar or bass or drum, or sang because of my photos, everyone who has bought or licensed a
photo (thank you!), to everyone who signed an act, recorded and released L.A. bands and saved
them from aural obscurity (Lisa Fancher/Frontier and Suzy/Patrick/Greg Shaw/Bomp, David/
Rand/KK/Dangerhouse, Rhino (especially Harold Bronson and Gary Stewart), Greg/Kim/Artifix,
Posh Boy, et al, thank you, plus all the writers and the magazines (especially *Creem*), fanzines
(*Back Door Man*, *New York Rocker*, *Punk*, *Slash*, *Lobotomy* and all the others, plus those who stole
my photos back in the day), the fan clubs: thank you all. Most of all, thank you to everyone I ever
photographed, who dazzled me with a live performance, or hung out at a punk gathering or party
in amazing clothes and having fun, in this book or in my files. I wish I could bring you all alive in a
series of books. To dream the impossible dream.
    Kudos and appreciation to everyone at Rizzoli/Universe, especially Charles Miers and my
patient and supportive editor, Jacob Lehman.
    Finally, eternal gratitude to my mother, who always encouraged my creativity, intelligence,
and curiosity, but worried about my excess energy. I needed all the energy I could muster to take
these photos and re-emerge decades later to share them with the world. Top of the world, Ma!

Ball of Fire

Before I ever met Jenny Lens I was told, "she's a ball of fire" — and this was from the renowned underground rock historian and entrepreneur Joe Carducci, of the Black Flag offices and SST Records. He's met a lot of crazy and wild punks, and he had only talked to Jenny — he hadn't even met her yet! He contacted me because he thought Jenny could use my help in revamping and reawakening her original punk photography archive, a treasure trove that had remained mostly dormant for the last twenty-plus years while she was involved in some horrible life. Of course, I knew of some of Jenny's work from the old days, so I was happy to give her a call out of respect, and to see how I could help her out.

After our first conversation and a quick perusal of her website, I knew that something cool was going to come of this introduction. Over a series of long calls, I answered questions and described my business M.O. to an always appreciative, incredibly respectful, and ultra-sensitive fifty-five-year-young punk-rock woman. Within only a few days of her sharing more photos with me and hearing her passion for the people she shot, I knew I was going to have to find this "ball of fire" a book deal.

My first book, *Fuck You Heroes*, had a lot of impact on those cultures I am so deeply associated with. It inspired the production of an award-winning documentary, and a Hollywood movie that most of us are embarrassed about. I am proud to say my book helped to keep some part of the culture and people's interest in it alive and kicking. It developed into my "Fuck You All" photo exhibition, which has traveled to many of the greatest cities around the world. But I know — and you know, if you're picking up this book in particular — that my book was not a complete history.

A few people were upset at the lack of female representation in my book, and made point to tell me about it. The truth is that my book covers the period of "hardcore" in skating, punk rock, and hip hop. During that time, the impact females made directly as leaders among the scenes was not particularly significant, so I've had to take some shit from some folks who thought otherwise. But it was my vision of my period of time.

Now we come to Jenny Lens, dubbed by none other than Patti Smith "the girl with the camera eye," the perfect prequel in punk to my "heroes." Jenny shot almost exclusively what I didn't; I wish I could have been working when she was. She's about ten years older than I am, so she had the opportunity and the interest to shoot many of the artists who inspired us before we became a part of the scenes we had only revered from afar. And she did it in a very personal way that I admired; only a friend of the people she shot could have taken so many of the images she did, from the stage, backstage, at parties, in the streets — even poolside with Joey Ramone. Not just anyone could do that.

The "hardcore" scenes were more than a few years away when she began. The seeds were being sown for all of what was to follow, and this innocent — or maybe not so innocent — woman was getting shots every day and in every way she could. Jenny considers herself a photojournalist more than a photographer. An acclaimed, degreed artist who never studied photography, her ego wouldn't let her pose people. Like myself, those around her inspired her to work hard. She's got some great photos of early punks who inspired me, who I never saw in those really early days — when punk was still just really fun. The truth is, I was a little too young and naive to be out in the clubs at that time, but I was reading the 'zines and I always noticed that photo credit (when it wasn't forgotten) by that girl Jenny Lens . . . I thought she must really have been focused on her photography to have given herself that name — I wasn't that dedicated yet!

I finally met Jenny in person 2005, when she came to my book-signing event in Los Angeles. She was incredible in person: bright magenta Shirley Temple curls, looking healthier than she did in her photos from twenty-five years earlier. Since then she had become a raw foods vegan, and in re-opening her archives and picking up communication with so many people who began to share the passion of her work via the internet, she had gained a renewed vitality for life. Even as she juggled constant commissions and photo requests from international publications, she was dealing with the painful memories of her punk years, the people gone, the bootlegged photos, the hard times, the lack of money — and she refused to let that stop her.

So here it is. We got her the book deal, and I became her mentor, an honor and a pleasure. Ladies and not so gentlemen, I present to you: Jenny Lens.

— Glen E. Friedman, 2007

A Punk, a Nose, and a Camera

My first exposure to punk was in the winter of 1976. I grew up in Glendale, a suburb in the east L.A. valley area. I danced to *American Bandstand* (and what a thrill when Jenny later took me to shows!) and the *Real Don Steele Show* made for some fun times and instilled in me my love of music. The Sugar Shack, in North Hollywood, was a teens-only hangout, where you'd always run into Joan Jett and other future punk superstars on the dance floor. That is where I learned of new fun bands with outlaws and girls who had razor-sharp attitudes who, in most cases, were tougher than many of the guys hanging out with them. The Shack introduced me to this very underground music, first glam/glitter and then punk and its roots. Punk in those days meant all kinds of musical influences.

D.J. Chuckie Star spun local bands like the Runaways and the Quick (who opened for the Damned in April, 1977). When you heard the first notes of "Cherry Bomb," you grabbed the person next to you and ran out on the dance floor and gave it your best Cherie Currie/Joan Jett attitude. You often forgot anything else that was happening around you when you heard the pounding of Sandy's drums, Jackie's deep bass chords, Joan's hot rhythm playing, the raunchy, less-than-perfect guitar of Lita, and Cherie screaming, "I'll give you something to live for . . . have you, grab you, 'til you're sore!" They made us feel that we could be rock stars, too — we could be as bad-assed and as outspoken as we wanted to be!

I found my friends in the strangest places: the Capitol Records swap meets, alleys behind the X-rated Pussycat theater, hanging out after shows. But I found a lifelong friend because of my nose. On April 27, 1977, I hitched down Santa Monica Boulevard to see the Nuns at the Starwood, a local Hollywood club owned by gangster Eddie Nash. I had seen the Nuns the night before and I wanted more. Someone grabbed my T-shirt. I looked down, saw a finger and a camera pointing at me, and an intense face looking me straight in the eyes and yelling, "Your nose *ruined* my Nuns shots last night!" The rest is history.

It was because of Jenny that I got to see so many great bands, not just punk bands but others — Led Zeppelin (Jenny: he got so stoned that he slept through them, in ninth row center seats! I kept running up to him, yelling, "Boring! They are soooo boring! Wake up, do you know how much I could have sold that ticket for?"), Alice Cooper's promo appearance (I talked to him, but Jenny hasn't found those

negatives, darn it!), and many more. Punk was our scene because we made it our way and no one had any power over us. The Ramones, the Damned, the Germs, Go-Go's, X, Screamers, Weirdos, writers, and the fans who made it happen: anytime they saw Jenny coming, it was natural for them to expect Jenny was going to flash her camera and do what she did naturally — make art. There were so many times when Jenny didn't have a dollar to her name, but somehow her presence and her camera were there to capture moments and events that others only wish they could have experienced.

I am lucky. I was this skinny eighteen-year-old Chicano kid who would do anything to help Jenny, because I was without a buck, too. I helped wind film, label photos, file, or roll joints. We sold buttons that we hand-lettered using big, brightly colored markers on black-and-white Xeroxes of her photos. That's when Jenny starting telling me I had talent and had to become a graphic artist. When we started working on this book, she asked me if I had ever thought, when she pushed me back then to become a graphic designer, that it was so I'd eventually design her book? Nobody else ever pushed me toward an art career the way she did.

Jenny stood up to people, and her artistic temperament and integrity were neither appreciated nor understood by most. Her camera was her life. She didn't get paid for ninety-five percent of what she did, she didn't drive a fancy car (we once drove up to the Playboy Mansion and the valet shook his head at her dirty Chrysler New Yorker), she didn't wear fancy clothing (she owned maybe five either homemade or thrift-shop dresses in the four years she shot), and all she got were photo passes (for which she often had to beg) and sometimes a rare house tab (which she would give to me). You couldn't live off that then and you can't now. So many of the people in her photos have gone on to great things. The Go-Go's graced the cover of *Rolling Stone*, played to tens of thousands of kids around the world, set fashion trends and were the first all-girl group to do what they did. But we knew them before they ever formed a band. Jenny captured these early pieces of history that remind us of the cutting-edge passion, the risks we took that changed music, fashion, and the people who made it.

Now the world can see just a tiny fraction of what Jenny Lens has given to those personalities on and off stage. She has given immortality to so many, some famous, some forgotten, some legendary, all through her camera eye. These

April 26, 1977, the Nuns at Starwood. The photo that launched our enduring friendship.

June 1, 1979, at Fiorucci's in Beverly Hills. Mark embraces life so fully. I always thought Divine and John Waters were hugely influential regarding early punk style and attitude.

photos are a timeless and important part of rock history. Jenny Lens and her artistic eye — what she saw through the camera — are as much a part of rock history as the artists who performed the music. Unlike so many others now proclaiming that heritage, Jenny worked hard and was published more than any other early L.A. punk photographer. She managed to party, to dance and sing all night, to shoot, and still to be published, all without money and without even knowing what she was doing beyond following her heart and her instincts.

Punk Pioneers is Jenny Lens's long-awaited first solo compilation. She continues to struggle (editing the book tore her apart, having to omit so many photos and stories). After all these years of neither being paid, credited, nor appreciated — except by the fans who know her work but not her name — this is our gift to you. Jenny wanted me to have the chance to design the book of our shared memories. She knew it had to be in chronological order, and she relied on me to "make it flow and be dynamic." I wasn't sure if our friendship could survive it. But true to her promise and confidence it worked out, and we're better friends for it. That's Jenny — always standing up to people, in her confrontational but well-meaning manner, arguing until the very end. How she gets the energy to fight all the time and still make art is a mystery. Things don't come easy to Jenny. Except for making art.

I am honored to be part of history, part of this art, and most importantly, to have a great friend (I call her my sister) in Jenny Lens.

Thank you.

— Mark A. Martinez, 2007

Punks climbed on to the billboard on Sunset near Crescent Heights and spray-painted this — still relevant today — circa 1977.

The Girl with the Camera Eye

Or, how did a nice Jewish girl like myself ever document punk rock, changing not only her life but those of countless others? *Punk Pioneers* attempts to share a few of the sights and stories behind the earliest days of punk rock, when it first spread from New York to Los Angeles, San Francisco, and England. Coincidentally, the Ramones were the first and most significant band to tour and the first band I ever shot, and the Clash the last. In between those shows, four years passed that changed world culture forever.

As a young child, I grew up without much culture — no radio, minimal television, and few popular magazines. My photojournalistic style was closer to Weegee's: natural, spontaneous photos, the kind of photos taken quickly on the street, literally capturing real life as it unfolded in front of me. I made art and pretty much lived at the public libraries and the CSUN college library. I got into Elvis when I first heard the Beatles — not "I Want To Hold Your Hand," but their first release, "Please, Please Me." I listened to AM radio: KHJ, KFWB, and KRLA. Rock, surf, Motown, soul, Phil Spector's Wall of Sound's prolific releases, the British Invasion, Summer of Love, and more. I heard one-off hits from now-forgotten bands often cited as early punk inspirations — "Louie, Louie," "96 Tears," and "Pushin' Too Hard."

I will never forget humming and singing a popular song during high school lunch, and finding that another girl was surprised I was into rock. I was so shy, in my own little world. I was smart and talented, energetic and willing to say anything at any time. I was also fat and Jewish, so I was always the outcast. When my MFA project was on display at CalArts, I overhead another female student tell a male student that I didn't look like my art. People were amazed at my art, but confused that I had made it. Weight has always been an issue in my life. People were knocked out by my work being so overtly feminine — they'd look at my art,

Pandora's Box and other legendary Sunset Strip rock clubs. I was always attracted to the darker side of life, to film noir, man's cruelty to mankind and fate's cruel streak. I'm sure that being a first-generation American Jew born after the Holocaust, plus H.U.A.C., the blacklisting of loyal, patriotic film-makers and other innocent citizens, put me in a perpetual state of shock at America's hypocrisy. My favorite TV was either *Alfred Hitchcock Presents* or noir films like *Nightmare Alley*. I watched musicals — *Cover Girl* is my all-time favorite, about a woman torn between her musical career and the man she loves who wants her to quit the stage. I went to Teenage Fairs at the Hollywood Palladium, and during college to a few parties in Hollywood. But I was always making art, and I never had the time or the money to see a lot of great shows. Go out or make art? No choice, art comes first.

Do you think Annie Leibovitz or Jim Marshall inspired me? No — Martha Swope. I grew up on *Newsweek* and *Time* magazines. Despite that upbringing (or in spite of it), I'm a radical, progressive, hippie earth-mother punk. I longed to be the woman who had photographed all the Broadway shows and dancers, ballet and modern. I thought anyone who could stand that close to all these great performances and shoot them as they happened had to lead a very special, magical life. But Broadway? Ballet? Snowy, rainy, cold New York? Not quite my thing. I was a product of the most exciting rock eras. As a young teen, I studied *The Pictorial History of the Talkies*, my first movie history book. It is chronologically ordered — every year with a grid of black-and-white images of former stars. Those old movies weren't shown on television or in local theaters, and I was fascinated by those images. It's no coincidence I love to lay my photos out in a grid!

I never studied photography. I loved making things with my hands, and the camera felt alien and cold to me. I always received acclaim for my art, no matter the media. I earned a BA in Art from CSUN. I wanted to teach college art someday, so I earned my MFA in Design at CalArts just for the diploma. I was determined not to sit on my fat ass by myself making art. But what to do? I took low-end jobs until one day I saw a photo of an androgynous woman in *People* magazine — a simple snapshot that changed my life. Who was this strange woman quoting Rimbaud? "Jesus died for somebody's sins, but not mine." The moment I heard Patti sing that in "Horses," in November, 1975, I was hooked. My life was changed irrevocably, in ways I am still discovering.

I found out about the punk scene as it was happening in Los Angeles and across the nation with my local *Back Door Man* and *New York Rocker* fanzine subscriptions in the winter of 1975. I met Phast Phreddie Patterson, the editor

then they'd look at me and wonder. I was also marginally involved in feminist art. "Jenny Stern," my birth name, is on the wall of Judy Chicago's "Dinner Party." I had the choice of continuing to submerge myself in the "Dinner Party" or to pursue my passion for punk. I've never been a follower, so it was an easy choice.

I listened to music and watched old movies as a teenager, when I began to take art seriously. Dr. Demento's FM broadcasts introduced me to the wildest, dirtiest, earliest, and most recent releases, and added to that mix was my lifelong love of Broadway show tunes. I listened to Stephen Sondheim's *Company* and *Follies* (I am one of the very few to have seen the L.A. productions), and *A Little Night Music*. I saw Ginger Rogers in *Hello Dolly* when I was sixteen, *Mame* on my eighteenth birthday, and *Gypsy*, both with the incomparable Angela Lansbury. Seeing Marlene Dietrich or Angela Lansbury was as memorable as seeing Patti for the first time. *That* was my photography education: formal art classes, old movies, old movie books, musicals, many happy hours at the L.A. County Museum of Art, and falling asleep to modern art books, dreaming of Odilon Redon, Renoir, and Chagall.

I didn't drive until I was eighteen, so I missed the Doors at the Whisky, although I longed to see them. Another classmate always told me about her adventures at and head writer of *Back Door Man*, as the sun came up at the Capitol Records swap meet in the spring of 1976. I threw my first *Back Door Man* party in August that year. Phred tapped me on the shoulder for a shot of Martha of the Motels as I shot them at the Starwood in September, 1976. I argued with Phred that he hadn't seen the photos yet, how did he even know they would turn out OK? He told me they would be fine, and those photographs that ran in the October, 1976 issue launched my publishing career.

Around that time, however, *Back Door Man* also published a letter that described me in very hurtful, unflattering terms. Years later, when I reached out to reconnect with Phred and Don Waller, each wrote touching emails apologizing for their youthful misdeeds. I long ago forgave them, because they had simply kicked me in the butt to grow up. I always appreciated their friendship and support. Although it hurt at the time, I was too strong, too determined, and too obsessed with punk and with photography to let that stop me from hanging out with them and photographing them.

My goal as a photographer was threefold: to promote the bands I loved and help them succeed; to turn others onto the scene that I loved so much; and to document this cultural revolution for those who came after us. Photographs had saved my lonely life, so I shot everything I could, praying my photos would give solace and inspiration to others. I knew the healing power of art, and having lived through so many musical eras, I knew punk would make an impact and burn itself out quickly. Act now or the moment is gone forever.

How and when did Jenny Stern become Jenny Lens? I never thought about changing my name as a "commitment to photography." I never wanted to be a photographer and fought against turning it into a business. I turned down many high-paying, highly visible photo gigs because I didn't like the music, the actor or the performer. I was such a good student and daughter all my life. I never had fun like other teenagers, so it was now or never. How could I go corporate, deal with the straight working world and at the same time keep my integrity and embrace punk? I had no plans to keep shooting beyond the first few years when punk was exciting and new. I knew it would transform into something else, and I didn't want to be stuck shooting boring groups or, as it turned out, being stepped on in hardcore.

I wanted a punk name, like Tomata du Plenty of the Screamers or Exene, John Doe, or Billy Zoom of X, Cherie the Penguin or Tony the Tiger. But I never would have guessed a hateful taunt from Farrah Faucet-Minor would rechristen me as "Jenny Lens." Fans of X's "Los Angeles" are always surprised to hear it's about a real woman and her real personality. Exene, John, Jade Zebest (who created the early L.A. fanzine, *Generation X*), Alice Bag, and many others witnessed Farrah's outbursts against some of them, others (including the Dictators), and myself. One night, during one of Farrah's drunken rants, out flowed "Jenny Lens." The woman who delighted in tormenting me also gave me the most perfect name. Moral: you never know what good will come from someone trying to destroy you. What doesn't kill you makes you stronger.

Everyone is in pain these days, but early punks came from dysfunctional families, boring or difficult school lives, and were outsiders either by choice or surroundings. I can be deeply cynical, and my anger quick and fierce at times, which surprises people because I always appear so cheery. I always say, "Well, what do you think attracted me to punk?" Why am I drawn to film noir and the underbelly of life, while still wanting to lift people's spirits? Not all good guys wear white hats, nor bad guys black hats. Life is shades of gray.

I often felt anti-Semitism directed toward me: my family being turned away from a hotel because of our last name, "Stern"; my brother beaten at school; me forced to sing Christmas songs in my tone-deaf voice; being accused of killing Christ, and of more sins beyond my knowledge and control. These issues may seem petty to some, but being Jewish in a small WASP valley community was not easy, especially in a resentful post-war climate. Some felt that had it not been for the Jews, Hitler would not have involved the U.S.A. in the war. The irony is that I can't fit in with most Jews. I'm too radical, too far off the grid. Yet I embrace the ethics behind it. I was stunned to realize that Jews from New York, L.A., and

Tomata drew a heart with "Mom" on my arm after Farrah's good-bye party, September 17, 1977.

Blondie's Chris Stein and Debbie Harry, backstage at the Whisky, April 14, 1977; and Iggy Pop at the Santa Monica Civic Auditorium the next night.

I love this shot by Michael Yampolsky. This is exactly how I felt: introverted, intense, alienated, neurotic, and camera-shy. Although it looks like I hacked my naturally curly hair, blame it on the lack of conditioners available back then for curly girls. The photo cut off my favorite button that read: "Show Some Emotion."

Patti Smith in San Diego, November 11, 1976. As Flea described the photograph: "Patti as the glowing goddess she is."

England started punk. Who knew so many Jews were behind the earliest days of punk?

Hippies preached love and peace, yet I never felt accepted among my peers. I was sent home for wearing anti-Vietnam peace buttons, but why weren't more of my fellow high school peers protesting? I always thought hippies were hypocritical. Punks were far more inclusive regarding societal-defined differences than others, but we were certainly not one big happy family. We were the bright, creative outcasts, brought together because as misfits, our social skills were often offensive, defensive, and youthful. We "did our own thing" before that became a marketing phrase.

In 2007 I attended the local premiere of a highly fictionalized movie based on Darby Crash and the Germs. I was thrilled when I ran into someone in line who immediately recognized me. Many years ago this person turned to me at a time of

need, feeling suicidal. The person came to my apartment knowing not only that I would listen and be supportive, but that we could find reasons to live no matter how down we get. That person left in a renewed and inspired attitude because of my ability to relate and offer guidance and counsel. I lived across the street from Tower Records, a stone's throw east of the Roxy and the Whisky, so most everyone knew where I lived. I don't remember that at all, but it's not the first time I've heard a story like it. People tell me they met me in San Francisco and I offered them a place to sleep in L.A., and that they never forgot their time at my apartment. Imagine four years of constant shows and parties, working so hard on the photos, and meeting and talking with so many people. I don't remember all my good deeds. I had no idea I had left such an indelible and positive mark on so many lives. A nice Jewish girl indeed, but one in deep pain — pain which also caused me to flee just when I should have stayed.

My reaction to ignorance, hatred, and prejudice is to be as kind as I can. I apologize to those who are on the receiving end of my anger, my pain, and my impatience, but it's never without provocation. I've always been grateful to Farrah for my name, but puzzled as to why she said what else she said. Is it simply what Belinda says in her intro to "Mercenary" in *Beyond the Valley of the Go-Go's*: "The next song is the slowest and saddest song of the set. It's about a girl who likes to be mean. I know that I like to be mean. I know Charlotte likes to be mean. Who doesn't like to be mean? You tell me." Well, I don't like to be mean, and I always feel guilty about it. I'm a punk Blanche DuBois, Tennessee Williams' doomed heroine in *A Streetcar Named Desire*. "Some things are not forgivable. Deliberate cruelty is not forgivable. It is the one unforgivable thing in my opinion and the one thing of which I have never, never been guilty."

I don't like to be photographed and often hid behind others. In February, 1977, I drove Tomata du Plenty, the Screamers' lead singer and good friend of Joey and Dee Dee, plus Arturo Vega, the Ramones' art director, David Moon, and Joey Ramone to Little Tokyo. I have fun shots of them looking through Japanese records and toys, back when Japanese culture was still underground. I got excited when I saw a large statue with its fist in the air, just like Joey onstage. It wasn't until recently that I found out it's a soda machine in the form of Kamen Rider. Moon took a shot of all of us, me with my big "Jewfro," naturally curly hair, my handmade flowered blouse with calico trim. Not your idea of punk? Get over it. For us, it didn't matter what you looked like.

I quickly started to paint my face à la Matisse and his fellow Fauves. I really enjoyed my wild makeup, and pins and jewelry I either made or found at thrift stores. I wore either a little cotton slip with thrift-shop kimonos or a hand-sewn black dress for the next four years, until I picked up some thrift-shop square-dancing rockabilly dresses. I always created my own clothes from scratch. I was often criticized for being unprofessional because I wore the same dresses over and over. But I had neither the time nor the money to take all the photos I wanted to take, so clothes were not a priority. My focus then, as now, was about the photos and the history I was documenting.

On January 14, 1978, I shot the Sex Pistols at Winterland in San Francisco. My flash was damaged in the car ride up ("a thousand clowns" in a little Volkswagen). Robbie "Posh Boy" Fields introduced himself to me. I was always surprised anyone knew who I was — I was shy, and wanted to be invisible. My friend Gaby Berlin remembers him chasing me around while I giggled all night, until we ended up on the balcony. My flash wouldn't work, so why not mess around with him? He was so cute and charming in those days.

In *Hardcore California*, Craig Lee quotes from "Slush," a *Slash* parody that incorrectly suggested "fashion models would shove a Hostess Snowball in photographer Jenny Lens' ass." I remember that so well because while I was pushing the poseur models aside, K.K. and others were flinging spaghetti all over the kitchen floor. I was mad I missed those photos! The late Herb Wrede gave me two proof sheets and I'm in nearly every other shot, and Melanie Nissen took a few shots of Robbie and I making out in the closet after I fled from the models. John Ford is one of my favorite directors, and his *Liberty Valance* is just about the most perfect movie: "When the legend becomes fact, print the legend."

My last party — what a way to go — was in England in June, 1980, with the Pistols, X, the Go-Go's, Darby, Jordan, and even Farrah. My sparkly make-up was smeared because I was constantly on the move, seeking out photos, always hot and sweaty. (Darby told me to splash cold water on my face. I thought that would remove my make-up, but it worked, when I wasn't too busy to find water.) My magenta hair photographed red. I'm not one to primp. Once I left home, I worked and worked and never thought about my face. Almost all of my fabulous rock pins, buttons, and homemade or vintage jewelry were stolen when I left Hollywood. My best movie books were stolen, too.

One goal of this book, and of my online presence, is to inspire some to dig further, because "attention must be paid" before we are all gone. Those days were the most vivid, alive, and meaningful times in my life. Life was indeed easier because we could focus on making art and music. We didn't have the internet, so we had to hit the streets, when rents were low and traffic was quiet, and going out every night was quite possible even if you had little money.

I'd love to tell more stories, but this is a photo book, so I'll let my images speak for themselves. I chose the photographs in these pages because they were published long ago or became recent hits, or because they have great personal meaning for me, or to inform and educate many who think punk is all about mohawks and mosh pits. We saw and listened to a wide range of musical styles, visual and aural. I've included many photos that some might not think are punk. I shot when punk was fun! We L.A. women were as important, influential, and powerful as any of the better-known men. We were the punk Ginger Rogers, who did everything Fred Astaire did but backwards and in high heels. Before hardcore.

"Something's lost, but something's gained . . . I really don't know life at all."
— Joni Mitchell, *Both Sides Now*

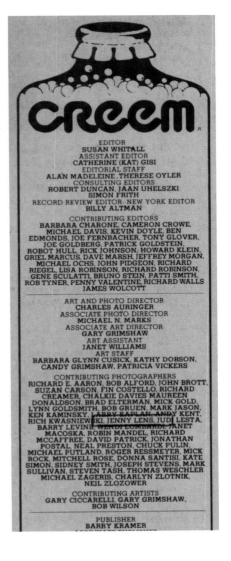

I never realized how quickly I became a highly respected photographer. I struggled so much because unsigned punk bands didn't bring in money or the advertising magazines needed. I was rarely paid, which was another reason I had so few clothes. I received letters from major magazines in America and Japan praising my work. It didn't mean much to me then, because the bands themselves rarely acknowledged me — it was always a struggle to get my name on guest lists and obtain press passes. I always felt like I was on the outside, working so hard but remaining invisible.

Music Life and *Rock Show* were major Japanese magazines. These are some of the earliest published photos of Devo, the Screamers, and the Weirdos. Although I knew Van Halen would be huge, I only took a few shots because punk was my life, not making money shooting bands I didn't like. My shots of the Rolling Stones were printed in Japan when the movie *Coming Home* was released. My greatest honor was being on *Creem*'s masthead. *Rolling Stone* was already too mainstream — *Creem* was *the* magazine we all read.

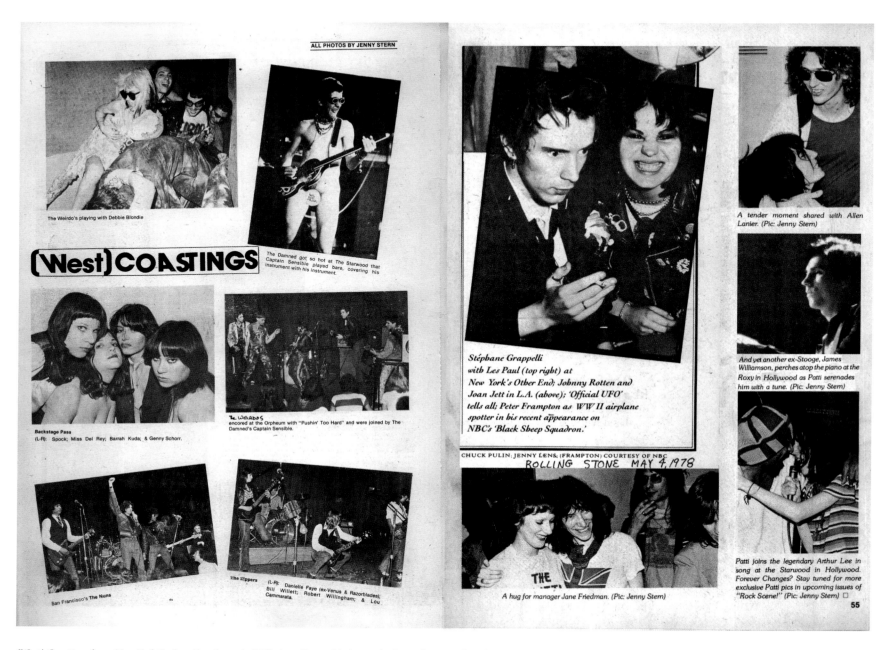

ALL PHOTOS BY JENNY STERN

(West) COASTINGS

The Weirdo's playing with Debbie Blondie

The Damned got so hot at The Starwood that Captain Sensible played bare, covering his instrument with his instrument.

Backstage Pass
(L-R): Spock; Miss Del Rey; Barrah Kuda; & Genny Schorr.

The WEIRDOS encored at the Orpheum with "Pushin' Too Hard" and were joined by The Damned's Captain Sensible.

San Francisco's The Nuns

The Zippers (L-R): Danielle Faye (ex-Venus & Razorblades); Bill Willett; Robert Willingham; & Lou Cammarata.

Stéphane Grappelli with Les Paul (top right) at New York's Other End; Johnny Rotten and Joan Jett in L.A. (above); 'Official UFO' tells all; Peter Frampton as WW II airplane spotter in his recent appearance on NBC's 'Black Sheep Squadron.'

CHUCK PULIN; JENNY LENS; (FRAMPTON) COURTESY OF NBC

ROLLING STONE MAY 4, 1978

A hug for manager Jane Friedman. (Pic: Jenny Stern)

A tender moment shared with Allen Lanier. (Pic: Jenny Stern)

And yet another ex-Stooge, James Williamson, perches atop the piano at the Roxy in Hollywood as Patti serenades him with a tune. (Pic: Jenny Stern)

Patti joins the legendary Arthur Lee in song at the Starwood in Hollywood. Forever Changes? Stay tuned for more exclusive Patti pics in upcoming issues of "Rock Scene!" (Pic: Jenny Stern) □

55

(West) Coastings from *New York Rocker*. Alan Betrock (RIP), founding publisher and editor of *New York Rocker*, first published the magazine in February 1976 and printed ten subsequent issues before Andy Schwartz took over in early 1978. I have early letters from Alan, in which he offered me my own column. I was too busy out shooting to be routinely sending in material, and I was already published in other magazines, but what an honor!

Johnny Rotten and Joan Jett in *Rolling Stone*, May 4, 1978.

Lisa Robinson's *Rock Scene*, which primarily covered New York and British bands, ran some of my Patti shots.

16

tiser in men's magazines. Three major distillers, leaders in the field, have signed new advertising schedules in the past year. Other major wine and spirits advertisers will be courted throughout the coming months.

Stepped-up sales efforts also are being directed at other categories well suited to OUI's upbeat male readership. Efforts to gain increased import-car advertising were begun with the recent introduction of a leading Japanese automobile manufacturer as a OUI advertiser.

In general, the advertising outlook for OUI is most encouraging, as the magazine's top four advertisers have increased their ad schedules for the coming year by 20 to 30 percent.

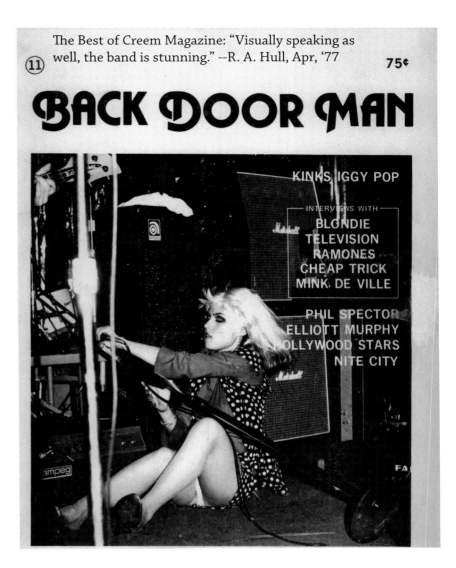

Punk rock, the "here today, gone today" phenomenon that author Ed Naha calls "the passing of an error," is blasted in a May '78 review of the nonmusical mayhem of those, like Patti Smith, who made it infamous.

Playboy's *Oui* magazine is gone, and Patti is still performing around the world. My Patti shot appeared in Playboy's 1978 Annual Report.

Blondie and *Back Door Man*, the cover that caused so much pain and so much fame. D.D. Faye saw this on my proof sheets and insisted over my objections that this was the perfect cover shot. Courtesy of the Back Door Man Collective (Phast Phreddie Patterson, Don Waller, Tom Gardner, and D.D. Faye), and the fabulous Debbie Harry.

Polydor used my photograph of the Jam in an advertisement for their tour of the United States in 1978.

18

I fell in love with Dee Dee Ramone's cheekbones when I first laid eyes on him in *Creem* magazine, and on the cover of their first classic release *The Ramones*. As an avid fan of old films, I studied the faces of the great movie icons in dozens of movie history books. Dee Dee was the most beautiful man I'd ever seen, with cheekbones to rival Errol Flynn, the best Robin Hood. I stood in line for hours to sit at Dee Dee's feet during their debut at the Roxy on August 11, 1976. The Roxy, more of an industry showcase than a dance club, made most of its money from food and drink and being comfortable for record company personnel and their buddies. It was hard to keep still, and thankfully the Ramones never played at another venue that required their fans to sit.

The next night I grabbed my camera simply because I wanted to shoot Dee Dee's cheekbones. I went to Hooper Camera in Granada Hills before getting on the 405 San Diego Freeway to drive south to the Roxy. The guys there told me what setting to use and I bought my first black-and-white film. I'd seen the late Richard Creamer holding his camera in the Ramones' faces the previous night and thought that so rude — playing and being hit with white light all night. Little did I know most punk shows would be so poorly lit I'd be forced to use flash too often.

I again arrived hours early and hung with other girls I'd seen around town. After the show they asked if I wanted to go to the Sunset Marquis, where the opening band, The Flamin' Groovies, were staying. I wasn't a fan, but thought, "Well, it's 2 a.m., what have I got to lose?" (Now I wish I knew what happened to those negatives!) I almost fell off the lobby sofa when "da brudders" walked in later, and their manager, Danny Fields, invited us up. Dee Dee was so sweet and accessible. I told him he was a brilliantly funny songwriter and asked him so many questions about the genesis of their songs — why a baseball bat, why 53rd and 3rd? He thought I was crazy and didn't understand my interest in his lyrics. He never believed me when I said they would be as big as the Beatles. I was stunned when he told me I was "the most normal girl he knew." I never met anyone like him.

I followed them down to the Smokestack, a.k.a. Fleetwood in Redondo Beach, the Golden Bear in Huntington Beach, and the Savoy in San Francisco.

I still have promo letters and flyers from the Savoy and the Smokestack, and Ramones fan club newsletters offering my photos for sale for three dollars each. I was thrilled: all my life I had been the outsider, and the Ramones let me follow them around, shooting them on and offstage, backstage, in hotel rooms, poolside, eating and just hanging out. I was intoxicated by the music, the daring clothes, the underground rock lifestyle, and all the great new people I was meeting.

I was neither alone nor lonely anymore, but blissfully happy, outside myself, taking in every glorious moment. I was floating, not eating, in constant motion and losing weight. *Creem* magazine wrote that the Ramones "were followed by a 250-pound cherub named Jenny." They added at least seventy pounds, so I never knew whether to be delighted I was mentioned or upset to have been reported that fat. Weight has always been such an issue for me: the clown outside, the sad, fat girl inside. But during punk, weight didn't matter — unlike the skinny 1960s. For years I constantly told everyone the Ramones were the next Beatles, whom I had seen when they first played the Hollywood Bowl in 1964. Patti turned me onto punk, but the Ramones were the turning point in my life. I floated for two weeks, as close to heaven as I'll ever get.

I didn't know Dee Dee washed several times a day. I have shots of him in the tub, but nothing X-rated! I could have made so much money and such a name if I had taken more adult-oriented or scandalous shots, but I'm a nice Jewish girl and I backed away from suggestions to take those kinds of photos. When *Spin*'s then photo editor, Lisa Corson, chose this shot of Dee Dee in a towel for his obituary, I asked why. She said, "He looked so sweet." Dee Dee *was* so sweet then.

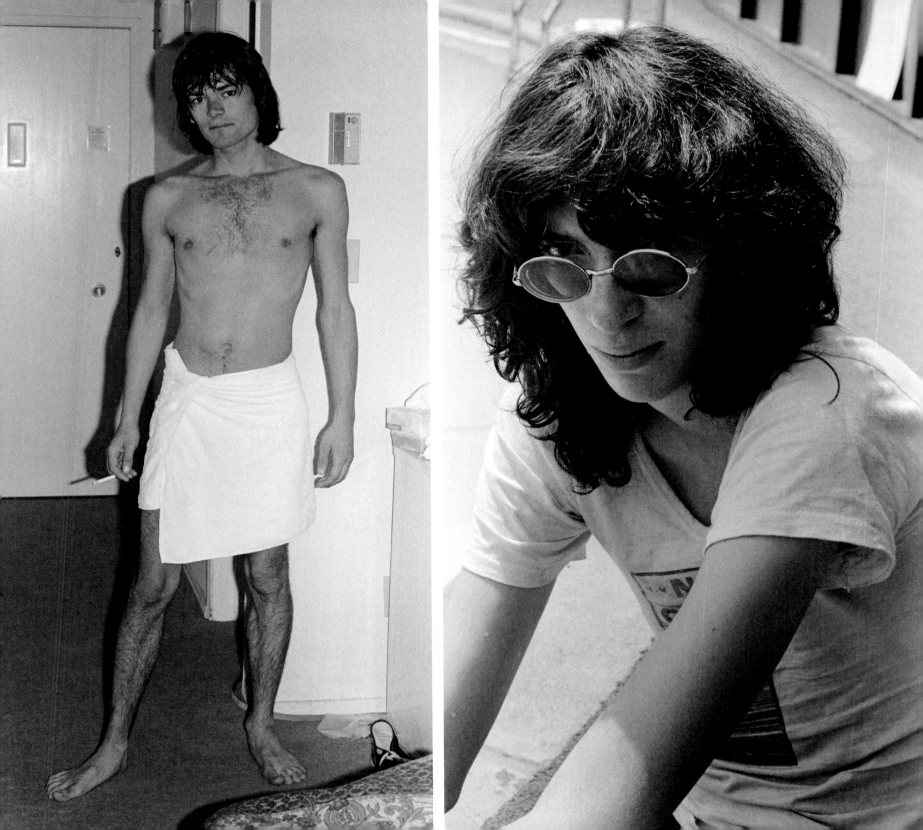

I love my Joey shots because you can see his face and his eyes, which he later covered with his long, thick hair. Beautiful, pale photos, soft and ethereal — capturing Joey's essence, hunched over, closed up, peering over his glasses with his constant far-away look, yet so introspective and vulnerable. All my Ramones photos reveal a youthful, optimistic energy at a time when they roamed freely among friends in sunny L.A. We all were sharing a once-in-a-lifetime adventure, making music, fanzines, parties, and memories that will live longer than we will. Our creations continue to inspire so many in ways none of us could fully imagine.

I flew up to San Francisco on August 19, 1976. Danny Fields recently told me that the band stayed in a "cheesy hotel on Van Ness." I thought it was next to a Chinese herbal warehouse — it's neither the Tropicana in Los Angeles nor the Phoenix in San Francisco. I shot Joey taking in the northern California sunshine wearing his "Carbona, Not Glue" T-shirt, lying by the pool, sitting and swimming. The shot of him lying by the pool is one of my most acclaimed and beloved shots. Mickey Leigh, Joey's brother, wrote that it was "one of [his] favorite shots of [his] brother." I always ask people why, because it's not my favorite shot (that would be Joey and Kamen Rider). They love his long bare legs, his Carbona T-shirt, but most of all, they love to see Joey, the quintessential New York punk, relaxing in the California sun.

Linda, Johnny's widow, told me that she didn't have shots of him smiling until she met me. Johnny Ramone led the way for tough men to be taken seriously when wearing T-shirts from Disneyland, which were at that time reserved for teens and little kids. Most T-shirts were plain or you'd create your own at the mall. T-shirt art and branding were still years away. The Ramones became role models who embraced comics and cartoons without being considered weird geeks because they were rock stars. They made all the outsiders feel cool and accepted. When relaxed and off in thought, Dee Dee had a perfect, classic, movie-star face. He is so beautiful in this shot (page 26): that's the Dee Dee whose cheekbones inspired me to pick up my camera and change my life. If not for Dee Dee's face, would I have ever taken rock photos? Highly unlikely. Check out his wrists: the knit fabric sewn onto his leather jacket was frayed. The Ramones were really broke. They also were among the first to wear T-shirts that were too small: belly-shirts for men.

During the fall of 1976, Zolar X rehearsed in my little rented cottage in the valley. I had no idea who they were, and years later I threw out my live shots from Osko's Disco basement. I never wanted anyone even to know I knew them. I was shocked when they became a cult band championed by Jello Biafra of the Dead Kennedys and then Sex Pistols' guitarist Steve Jones on his radio show, Jonesy's Jukebox. The sign on the wall behind them is from an art show, Anonymous was a Woman, at my alma mater, CalArts. I created the weaving, a hand-carved wooden table, and several sculptures behind them. My background was in art, not in photography. I rarely ever read a rock magazine.

I fondly remember a riotous birthday party I gave for Phreddie and his Back Door Man rascals on Halloween, 1976. He brought a dude named Ron to my house, who necked with me in my kitchen. It was Ron Asheton of the Stooges. I have more photos of him fondling me in a Nazi uniform the following week, before he went back to Detroit, where he'd immigrated with his brother Scott and a singer named James Osterberg (a.k.a. Iggy Pop). I had no idea who Ron or the Stooges were until I shot Iggy on April 15, 1977 — and only then did I understand why Iggy was so revered.

I snuck my camera in to see Patti Smith in San Diego on November 11, 1976, by thrusting my camera bag in Patti's late brother Todd's hands and telling him I'd meet him inside. I developed more than forty rolls of film incorrectly, hence the glow around Patti and her Fender Duo-Sonic guitar. The shot of Patti leaning back, her hair flowing down, was on the back cover of her Babel book, but credited to "Jenny Stern," my former name. The photo of her standing and holding her guitar has never been seen, it was taken immediately after she lay backward on the floor.

My camera was confiscated that night and I was escorted out by big, humorless security goons. I will never understand why, even today, people are not allowed to take photographs at rock shows. I was escorted out and my camera was removed again at the Santa Monica Civic Auditorium on May 12, 1978, right before Patti sang You Light Up My Life, carrying the American flag. I saw other cameras, but I sat and cried, my head in my lap. Who took those photos and where are they? If I had shot her, they'd be in this book.

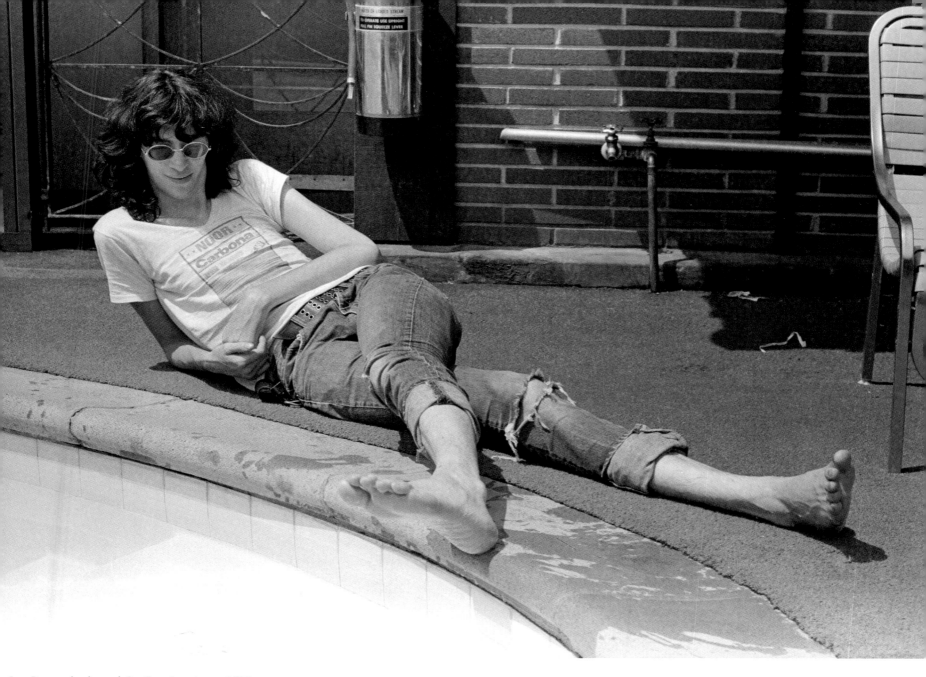

Joey Ramone by the pool, San Francisco, August 1976.

Following pages: Joey Ramone in swim trunks and towel, Orange County, August 1976, and at the first of many parties we threw for the Ramones. I created a sign, every word in a different color marker, thanking them for their magic, friendship, and music. I have shots of them in party hats, eating cake with streamers everywhere, for a backstage good-bye party.

Johnny and Dee Dee, Aquarius Records, San Francisco, August 1976.

Ron Asheton of the Stooges in his authentic Nazi uniform, November 6, 1976, as seen later in *Creem* magazine.

My Halloween, 1976 party with *Back Door Man* writers Audrey Pavia, Phast Phreddie, Don Waller, and Bob Meyers.

Above: Zolar X in my little cottage in the valley.

The Whisky was brought back to life by the emergence of international punk. Malcolm McLaren shows up quite often in my Ramones shots, first in their August 1976 debut shows, then in February 1977, and exactly a year later at the Masque Benefit. He knew famed glam groupie Sabel Starr (page 32) because she was the New York Dolls' Johnny Thunders' flame.

February, 1977 was memorable for Blondie and the Ramones. Blondie checked out the Whisky the night before their debut (I shot Rick Derringer that night), accompanied by Rodney Bingenheimer, who was L.A.'s biggest punk supporter. Blondie's L.A. debut was advertised in the *L.A. Times* as "Blondie with Tom Petty and the Heartbreakers." Debbie's wedding gown was spray-painted "T. P." She wore a wedding veil years before Madonna's memorable MTV Awards appearance. I love the beaded design, on the left, under the veil — her thrift-shop gown was gorgeous and disposable.

Debbie walked onto the stage wearing a Humphrey Bogart beige trench coat, black beret, and holding a New York paper announcing freezing weather. She pulled it all off to sing their first single, originally called "Sex Offender," which was renamed "X Offender" at the record company's insistence. I never understood why that was better. No one wore those kinds of boots unless they were in the flesh trade or in a French film. Shades of the Velvet Underground's "Femme Fatale" or "Venus in Furs."

I'm now *damned proud* that I took the *Back Door Man* cover shot that is now the cover of this book. I was banned from ever shooting Blondie again because of it, yet it garnered worldwide publicity for them. The photo that caused so much pain, then so much fame. It's now my most famous photo. If only I knew then what I know now . . .

I only saw famed rock writer Lisa Robinson twice, for the Ramones and Television. She was very kind to me when *Creem* ran that nasty bit about my weight. If only more people had paid heed to what she and Robert Hilburn were covering: punk. They were lone voices in the wilderness. I was too shy to ever submit any photos to the *L.A. Times* or to speak to Hilburn.

I shot Alice Cooper with Bernie Taupin, Elton John's lyricist, catching the Blondie/Ramones double bill a few days after the Blondie/Tom Petty show. Joey

Ramone was a huge Alice Cooper fan. I'd seen Alice at the Hollywood Bowl a few years earlier. Although I love theatricality, it was too posed, too staged, and neither dangerous nor exciting enough. I also felt it appealed more to teen boys, not to the eternal teen girl inside of me.

I remember when "Your Eyes" first hit the radio stations. I knew it would be a huge hit, but I never took Elton John seriously either. The flamboyant clothes and songs didn't do anything for me. I was into Joni Mitchell ("Ladies of the Canyon," "Blue," "For the Roses," and "Miles of Aisles" are still favorites) and Broadway composer Stephen Sondheim, whose masterpieces *Into the Woods*, *Sweeney Todd*, and *Assassins* were not yet written. I sang along to *Company*, *Follies*, and *A Little Night Music*. *Follies* is a great Broadway cult classic, but only a handful saw it in New York and even fewer in Los Angeles. What memories! I knew I was changing when I worked in my darkroom, printing shots of Patti Smith, instead of seeing *A Chorus Line* for the third time. "What I Did for Love" is my motto: about our love, devotion, and absolute commitment to the demands of the often heart-breaking creative life.

Joni and Sondheim, and some other Broadway musicals, were the only records I listened to prior to punk. I grew up on all the great rock of the 1950s and 1960s, but by the 1970s the radio was boringly dreadful. The only bright spot was Dr. Demento, who certainly inspired more punks than he is given credit for. The radio never played Iggy, MC5, the Velvet Underground, or the New York Dolls.

N.Y. in L.A. — the Ramones triumphantly returned to L.A. on February 16, 1977, at the Whisky, with playful and tuneful Blondie. It was hard to choose just these shots. As anyone who saw the Ramones in their early performances will attest, they were the best. I stood on the Whisky staircase, halfway up, halfway down, jumping up and down, dancing and screaming, pumping my fists in the air, and took tons of amazing shots. I had such close access and was privy to private conversations. I felt blessed that for once my life was exciting and meaningful.

The Ramones were loved in L.A. and they loved L.A., as my many backstage, party, and live photos go to prove. Rodney Bingenheimer was an early punk proponent, with his *Rodney on the ROQ* radio show and live shows at varied venues, such as the Bel Air Hotel and Osko's Disco. I was thrilled to accompany the Ramones and to shoot them with Rodney in the far background, and the band answering fan phone calls, choosing records, and Joey holding the home-made T-shirt. Notice the most popular poster of all time in the background: Farrah Faucet-Major's nipples, perfect teeth, and blonde curls. That's what we were rebelling against: society's definitions of beauty and culture, force-fed down our throats. We wanted to make our own music and our own stars.

I love this expansive shot of the Ramones backstage at the Whisky. Joey is wearing the T-shirt from their KROQ visit the previous night. I remember other photographers shooting in front of them. I felt I didn't have the right to be part of that elite group, so I shot from the sidelines. I love that Dee Dee is looking straight at me.

In spring, 1980, X were celebrating their Slash release, "Los Angeles." Exene's sister was killed in a car accident on the way to the show. John Doe smashed the window above the air conditioner. The club replaced the window, but shards of glass sat outside on top of the unit. When I took this shot, I didn't realize yet that the Whisky would become my all-time favorite place to shoot and to see shows. The upstairs backstage area was pure magic. It's also where I got pregnant, in the restroom. I didn't have the child. But how many women got pregnant in the upstairs bathroom, backstage at the Whisky?

I photographed Joey Ramone, Harold Bronson of Rhino Records, and Johnny Ramone standing outside Rhino Records on Westwood Boulevard. The valiant work of the legendary Rhino records store contributed to keeping so much of our culture alive. They imported the coolest British and hard-to-get punk, stocked old classics, and later kept the music alive by starting a phenomenal record company. They released so much great music for us to still enjoy. They were the first to package punk in their D.I.Y. series, and were the first to revive my archive and my career by using so many of my photos.

I can visualize Gary Stewart showing me bootlegs from their back closet. He later oversaw the production of most of those punk, power pop, new wave, and great classic rock packages. I met them all at the Capitol Records swap meet. I met more important, influential early L.A. rock and punk movers and shakers at that swap meet than anywhere. We'd stay up all night after a show and converge in darkness to find the best music, fanzines, and memorabilia, before the days of the internet. In those early days, if not for Harold, Gary, Lenny Kaye, Greg Shaw (of Bomp!), and the *Back Door Man* contributors, most of us would never have heard nor read about the coolest music ever recorded.

The Ramones and Blondie celebrated together at an infamous party at the Screamers' home. It was always affectionately called the Wilton Hilton because it was on Wilton, just south of Franklin, around the corner from the A.F.I. at Western. Either Tomata du Plenty of the Screamers or Arturo Vega, the fifth Ramone and the creator of their logos and merchandise, asked me to drive them to Little Tokyo with David Moon, the first live on-stage Pinhead. They and Joey Ramone wanted to explore those streets. I had never explored Little Tokyo either, although I was born and raised in L.A.

We literally fell upon this soda machine disguised as Kamen Rider. I got so excited and asked Joey to pose. These shots are so sweet and fun, playing with toys, records, magazines — and a glimpse of Japanese pop culture years before it was assimilated into American culture. There was a lot of anti-Japanese sentiment after the Second World War. It took the punk youth to bridge that gap. It took punks in their twenties to make watching cartoons and playing with Japanese toys acceptable and cool.

Blondie's Bel Air hotel room was a continuous open house. I didn't go to many shows or read rock magazines, but I certainly heard Queen on the radio. Rodney brought two older, well-dressed men to the hotel room. I extended my hand to the taller one, with dark curly hair and a gorgeous face. I said, "Hi, I'm Jenny," and he said, "I'm Brian." I backed out of the room, as if I had just met royalty. I was reacting to his British accent, thinking he must be someone. It was Queen's Brian May.

Punk broke down barriers with Queen's Brian May, Jimmy Destri, Chris Stein, Gorilla Rose, and Debbie on the bed talking to publicist Toby Mamis. Michael Wilcox, an L.A. guitarist, told me he ripped his pants and Debbie sewed them for him. Both my shots of drummers Clem Burke and Queen's Roger Taylor with Debbie were printed in *Creem* and *Music Life*, Japan. February 1977 was quite a month for me because I began to meet all the people I'd photograph who would become performers, writers, fans, and *the* movers and shakers of the scene.

The following December, 1977, Elektra Records hired me to shoot Queen with some record company personnel in a fancy Beverly Hills Hotel. I caught hell the next day because Freddie Mercury complained that I had asked them for their autographs. I still have my autograph books, fun little journals that bring tears of joy whenever I dig them out.

The one and only Runaways, Lita Ford and Cherie Currie. Not sure where I photographed Lita, but that photo stuns me. The classic rock goddess stance, glowing, with those glam space-age boots and her long hair. I shot Cherie at the Santa Monica Civic Auditorium when Cheap Trick opened for them on April 1, 1977. I had to sneak my camera in again, but what a classic shot. Plus a lovely, sweet fun backstage shot with Rick Nielsen, Tom Petersson, and Joan Jett.

Bomp Records store owners Suzy and Greg Shaw (RIP) on the store's opening day, April 9, 1977. I *never* wanted people to know they were being photographed. I tried to shoot what I saw, not poses. My shots are candid, true, spontaneous, and honest. I love seeing the Fab Four and my photos of the Ramones, Patti, Blondie, and others beneath them. I can see my handwritten note over Suzy's shoulder, describing my photos. Imagine that — my photos under photos of the Fab Four.

I met Blondie in a red padded booth at the Whisky on February 8, 1977, when Rick Derringer performed. The next night they made their L.A. debut opening for Tom Petty there, and for the Ramones the following week. Their manager Peter Leeds, on the left with the dark sweater and striped shirt, grabbed me and threw me out the following October. The bruises are gone, the mental scars will always remain. But I will always love Blondie.

Opposite: Famed glam groupie Sabel Starr and Malcolm McLaren, backstage at the Whisky during Blondie and the Ramones, February, 1977.

Following pages: Debbie Harry at the Whisky, 1977.

"X Offender"

Opposite: Debbie Harry at the Whisky, 1977.

L.A. Times rock critic Robert Hilburn (one of the few mainstream media champions of early punk) with writer Lisa Robinson and publicist Susan Blonde, both from New York, talking to Blondie publicist Toby Mamis, leaning over the table.

Bernie Taupin, Elton John's early lyricist partner, checking out the Ramones and Blondie with Alice Cooper.

Following pages: The Ramones at the Whisky, 1977.

No one championed punk more than Rodney, between his KROQ shows and his hosting and introducing bands at various venues. We often wore handmade T-shirts like Joey's "Rodney KROQ."

Dee Dee Ramone and Jenny Lens at the Whisky, with Johnny in the background. I'm wearing another of my homemade dresses from college with a white gardenia fabric flower.

The Ramones backstage at the Whisky, February 20, 1977. I love that Dee Dee is looking at me when the press and "official" photographers were standing directly in front of them. Looking through my archives, I was surprised to find so many detailed backstage shots of the Whisky, which quickly became my favorite place to shoot and hang out. I stood on the stairs dancing, screaming, and shooting all night, then dashed upstairs for the backstage shots.

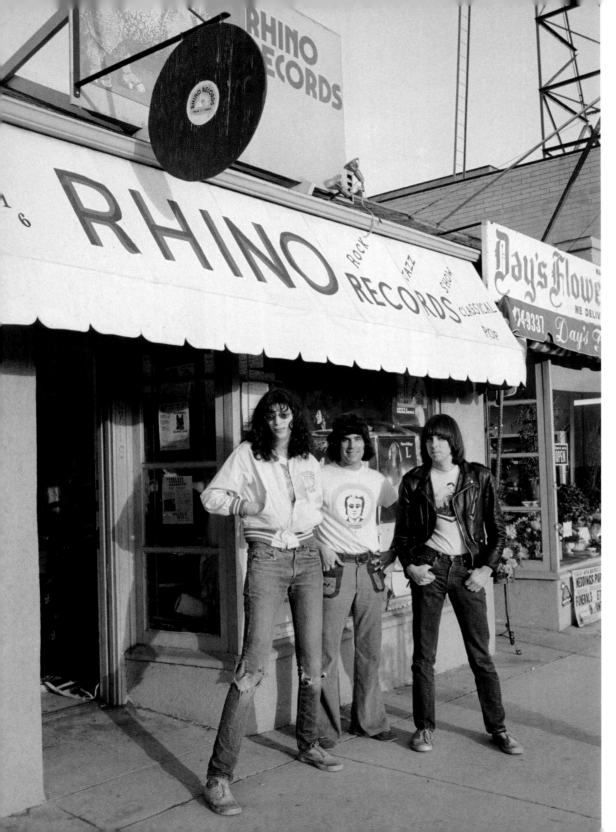

The legendary Westwood Rhino Records store: Joey, Rhino co-founder Harold Bronson, and Johnny.

Opposite: Joey and Kamen Rider, Little Tokyo, Los Angeles, February, 1977.

Following pages: Queen's drummer Roger Taylor kissing Debbie Harry while Brian May plays guitar, with assorted L.A. punks: Tomata du Plenty of the Screamers, Black Randy, Michael Wilcox, Gorilla Rose, Rodney, Phast Phreddie, Genny Body of Backstage Pass, Fayette Hauser, Blondie publicist Toby Mamis, and Blondie band members. Bel Air Hotel, February, 1977.

John Cale's birthday at the Starwood, March 9, 1977. I have shots of the Ramones visiting John with Jane Friedman, who managed John and Patti.

50

April Fools Day, 1977. Cheap Trick's Rick Nielsen in cap and bassist Tom Petersson kissing a smiling Joan Jett, backstage at the Santa Monica Civic Auditorium the night Cheap Trick opened for the Runaways.

Previous pages: The one and only Runaways, Lita Ford and Cherie Currie.

Bomp Records store owners, Greg (RIP) and Suzy Shaw, on their opening day, April 9, 1977. We all owe a debt of gratitude to them because their store was an invaluable resource during the early days of punk on the West Coast.

The Screamers were the most *perfect* band, especially to photograph. Live or posed, their collective talent continues to captivate those who've stumbled across them. I could write a book about them, fill it with photos and bootleg recordings, and still neither capture nor convey their allure, magic, appeal, or the hold they have on us after so many years. Long live the Screamers, the best band you never saw live.

Television's first release, *Marquee Moon*, became an instant classic for many of us. Most punk shows were poorly lit and required a flash. I love my magenta-tinged shot of Tom Verlaine lost in thought — the timeless, transcendent poet. Unlike the Screamers, Television were not an exciting band to shoot. I love Television, but they were very cerebral at a time that most of us on the West Coast preferred and needed to dance off our high energy. Despite the city's reputation, Los Angeles is not laid-back. The city of my birth is a tangled mess of neuroses, class struggles, poor public transportation, and crazy contradictions. We were angry, energetic, and enthusiastic. Raw, loud, fast music fed and released our creative passions.

A lovely, spontaneous shot of a very relaxed and celebratory Debbie Harry. I love her sparkly makeup, unusual for its time. Debbie and Chris encouraged me to publish my photos when I met them in February. When they returned to L.A., Debbie told me she was so proud of me because I had photos in *New York Rocker*. I didn't have the heart to tell her I had submitted the photos before I ever met her. She was so ambitious but so sweet to share her energy with me, and that's why I was so shocked and hurt by the *Back Door Man* cover controversy.

Debbie called me "Paparazzi Jenny" and signed photos to me with that nickname. I didn't know what "paparazzi" meant. It was a compliment, a term used in Fellini's classic film, *La Dolce Vita*, which I had seen back in college. I love Fellini's *Juliette of the Spirits*. I was among people who loved an underground culture that one found purely through instincts, not through networking of any kind. Only a few people, city folks with theatres or television stations showing foreign films, knew or loved Fellini then.

The Damned joined local punks at the Orpheum, a small venue designed for intimate plays. Captain Sensible spread out, while lead singer Dave Vanian, their manager and Stiff Records founder Jake Riviera, and guitarist Brian James shielded their faces from my camera. But these tall, dark, and very handsome men with strong features are readily recognizable.

Captain Sensible of the Damned joined the Weirdos during the Seeds' "Pushin' Too Hard." Robert Lopez of the Zeros is in the front row, on the right in a striped shirt. He is now El Vez, the Mexican Elvis who is a talented entertainer with his own amazing theatrical troupe and a vast musical repertoire. "Pushin' Too Hard" is a great garage rock classic. I remember hearing it when it first came out during the hippie era. Punk was inspired by all kinds of music: roots, rockabilly, blues, country, garage rock, soul, the Beatles and Elvis, Phil Ochs and Bob Dylan, Broadway and Tin Pan Alley. The Seeds aren't a household name, but are an L.A. band, and the Weirdos and Captain Sensible knew the roots of punk.

The Weirdos at the Starwood's V.I.P. tables upstairs, with diagonal wood paneling, April 17–18, 1977. Grace Roman, Dave Trout, Nickey Beat, John Denney and Cliff Roman. I often wished for a film crew. I'd look at the various tables and feel transported to Berlin of the 1920s. Marlene Dietrich meets *I Am a Camera* and *Cabaret* meets George Grosz and Otto Dix. Punk: Berlin in the 1920s, film noir, Theda Bara, Busby Berkeley, Ballets Russes, Symbolists, and all the art and music I craved and knew so well.

I constantly saw so many moving images and wished for video cameras. But I didn't have the money, so I took a lot of "key" frames, as if story-boarding a film. I hand-rolled film to save money. Unfortunately, light occasionally entered the film and you can see the effects in my shot of the Damned backstage at the Starwood — Captain Sensible, John Denney, Nickey Beat, and Cliff Roman. I lent the proof sheets and negatives to a friend. Someone dumped coffee on some of them. Ah, the punk life!

I gave my shot of Captain Sensible nude to their manager, Jake Riviera, who also managed Elvis Costello among others. It was published and turned into a best-selling button, though I never made a cent nor received credit. Captain Sensible bent over, butt naked, shirtless Dave Vanian, with Rat Scabies and Brian James leaving the stage and the Quick's drum kit above them. Local punks, my good pal Michael Wilcox and Mel Al, are in front of me. More than two decades later Michael Wilcox played with the Damned.

On May 3, 1977, two of my favorite performers, Dave Edmunds, along with his Rockpile partner, Nick Lowe, and their manager, Jake Riviera, visited Bomp. Their "pub rock" was a major influence for many bands, a factor in the rise of Stiff Records, Elvis Costello, and more. Tracks on Wax! I love this shot of Back Door Men Phast Phreddie Patterson, Thom Gardner, Dave, Don Waller, with Bill Inglot (Rhino and Time-Life's remastering sound producer for thousands of releases) and Suzy Shaw behind them. I also shot writers Gene Sculatti, Gregg Turner, and others at Bomp.

The Screamers on the bus bench is my most well-known L.A. shot. I had no idea what "666" represented when I took the photo. I love the palm trees, the man with the Bermuda shorts, my shadow on the far left and Pleasant Gehman's on the right. It was so much fun finding the little old lady with the neck brace, reading a scandal sheet. She put it down and held up Tomata's fave mag, which would soon be banned, and which inspired one of their best songs: "It's a Violent World (and you better get used to it!)." I could only take one shot because Tomata and Tommy thought she was so cute they started laughing. One shot, but what a great shot! Pure spontaneity — no stylists, no direction, just real life.

The Screamers made their debut at *Slash* magazine founder Steve Samioff's offices on May 28, 1977. Words cannot express what it was like seeing the Screamers. Pure art, like seeing a Van Gogh or a Picasso that you've stared at in books for years. But up close and personal, the colors, the textures, the reality of seeing great, classic art. Joyous, life-affirming, memorable, never to be repeated.

Punk bands often opened for Van Halen. Their manager, Marshall Berle, worked at the Whisky. David Lee was always funny and nice, but Eddie knew he was going to be a big star and didn't waste his time on me. David Lee loved joking and hanging out with the punks. I knew Van Halen would be huge, but I never shot the money shots — I just caught a few shows when I wanted to see the opening punk bands. So many of us loved the Mumps, a fun band with frienly members. The Mumps' lead singer Lance Loud was the first man to come out on American television, during the first reality series *An American Family* for PBS.

I shot Rodney introducing so many bands, quite often with more people onstage than on the floor. The genuine joy that he and Captain Sensible express in this photo was quite common. I appreciated Rodney, a generous spirit who has not been given the credit he earned and deserved.

The Screamers.

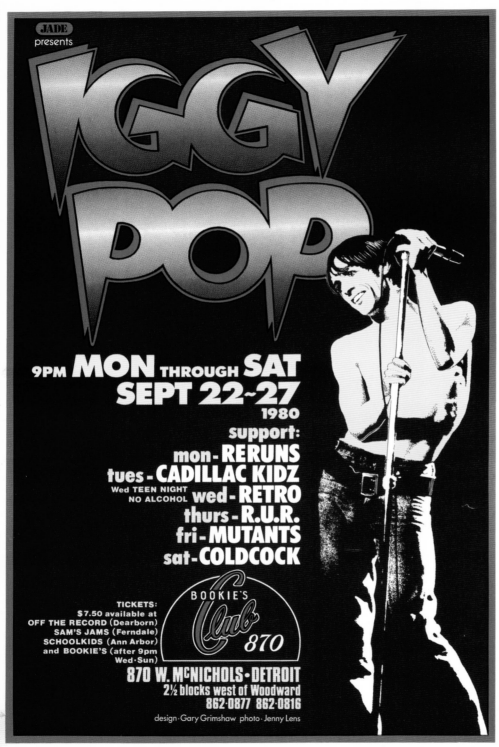

1013

Iggy Pop at the Santa Monica Civic Auditorium, April 15, 1977. David Bowie was on piano, but bathed in red light the whole evening and difficult to photograph. Blondie opened the show and Iggy played Ravel's Bolero between sets.

The Civic banned photographers on the floor, so I hid my camera. Hellin Killer, Mary Rat and I shared two folding chairs near the front. I didn't have a close-up lens, but a coupler that zoomed in but cut my light in half. So between the girls bouncing up and down on the chairs, no light, and no flash, I still managed to take quite a few really great shots.

Iggy loves this black-and-white shot and it was later used on a poster for his Detroit tour in 1980. Gary Grimshaw, the Associate Art Director at *Creem* magazine, found my photo in their files. I discovered the poster at a Pasadena record store in the mid-1990s (I had never seen it). It was chosen for inclusion in *The Art of Rock: From Presley to Punk*, one of the few books with my work in it that I don't own.

Previous pages: Tom Verlaine of Television and Debbie Harry, onstage and backstage at the Whisky on April 14, 1977.

Saturday April 16, 1977: Pleasant Gehman dared the Germs to get on the bill with the Weirdos. Pleasant, Dave Trout, Lorna Doom, Darby Crash, with Pat Smear on the floor. I might have the only evidence leading up to their landmark debut.

The Damned under the Bomp Records store sign. This was the defining week that gave birth to first-generation L.A. punk.

Opposite: Settling the rumor: Yes, the Damned came to the Orpheum as per the Weirdos' invitation.

The Weirdos and the Damned at the Orpheum and the Starwood, April 16–18, 1977.

The final Damned set at the Starwood, April 18, 1977. The *Herald Examiner* reviewer was not impressed with their debut show the first night. Captain Sensible whispered into my ear to pay attention. The Damned were not going to leave L.A. with a lukewarm review. They left a lasting impression.

Dave Vanian with gas mask and flare. I love the strange quality of this photo. Light entered when hand-rolling the film (and people were helping me, so I have no idea who or how this happened). The Quick's drum kit in the background is distilled into an abstract series of circles. That evening was surreal, magical, and strange, like this image.

Drummer Rat Scabies setting his drum kit on fire with the lighter fluid he often carried around.

Following pages: My infamous nude photos of Captain Sensible. The first British punk band to visit L.A. left their mark, on and offstage.

The Damned and Blondie's drummer, Clem Burke (a.k.a. Elvis Ramone) at the Screamers at the Wilton Hilton Damned Party, April 18, 1977.

Opposite: Debbe Harry with Jeffrey Lee Pierce of Gun Club (soon to become Blondie's Fan Club President, resulting in Chris and Debbie's tribute to him, "Under the Gun") and the Weirdos at Bomp Records, April 23, 1977.

The Screamers on the bus bench, Gower Gulch, spring of 1977.

Opposite: *Back Door Man*'s Phast Phreddie Patterson, Thom Gardner, and Don Waller, with Rockpile's Dave Edmunds outside Bomp Records, May 3, 1977. Behind them are Bill Inglot and Suzy Shaw.

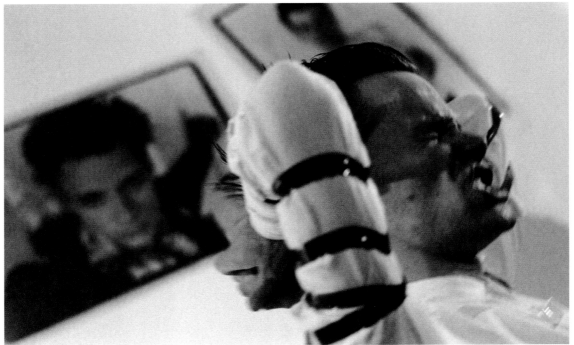

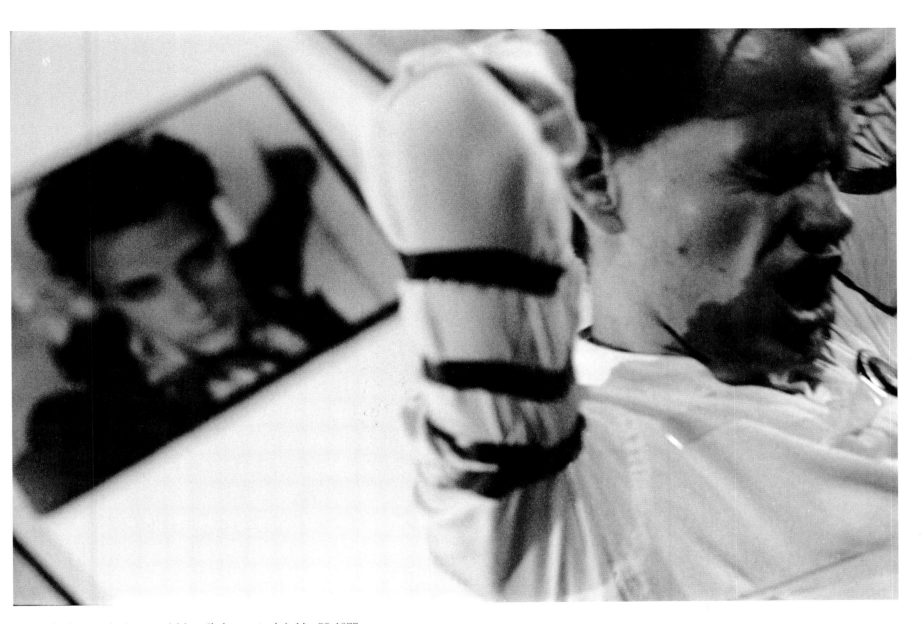

Tomata du Plenty at the Screamers' debut, *Slash* magazine loft, May 28, 1977.

Tommy Gear

Classic shot of the Screamers.

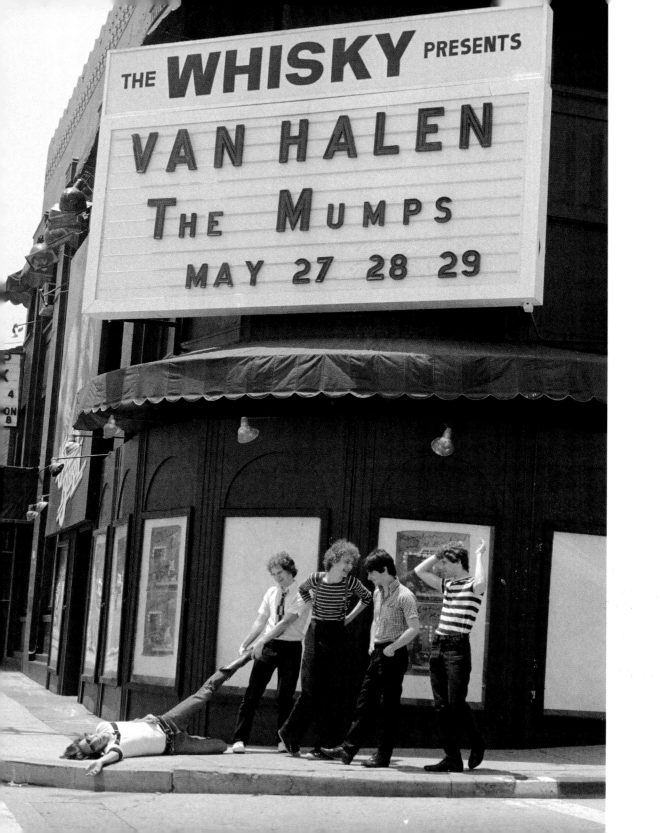

Van Halen's lead singer, David Lee Roth, comparing muscles with the Mumps' lead singer, Lance Loud (RIP), inspired by the Mumps' song "Muscle Men."

Alex Van Halen with David Lee Roth, Eddie Van Halen, and two others, dressed as punks outside of Tower Records.

Opposite: The Mumps beneath the Whiskey marquee, May 27, 1977.

The Germs' first official photo shoot in June, 1977. I'll never forget Pleasant's phone call, screaming so excitedly that she convinced *Slash* magazine to let her interview the band but that they didn't have any photos and were on their way over. The highlight was Pat and Darby rolling Lorna down the sidewalk in a small wire trash barrel, from which she emerged smiling and beautiful. They all got into the big trash bin behind the Roxy and posed with trade magazines over their faces. One had Joan Baez on the cover. Mark Martinez and Pleasant helped them out of the trash bin. Darby ran up a billboard, arms outstretched as if crucified, and jumped down before I could take more than a few shots. My favorite is the early published shot of the Germs with "Barbra Streisand" at the Licorice Pizza record store diagonally across the street from the Whisky. *Simpsons* creator Matt Groening worked there, Patti read poetry in the parking lot, kids always drank there before the shows — so many memories on the Sunset Strip!

Joan Jett, Exene Cervenka, Pleasant Gehman, Rand McNally, and John Doe at X's apartment on La Jolla, behind Circus Books (the inspiration for *Adult Books*). Rand and John played in the Randoms and Black Randy's bands. Rand, Black Randy, and the Screamers' drummer K.K. Barrett formed Dangerhouse Records. These spontaneous gatherings of early L.A. punks usually occurred after an evening at the Whisky or the Starwood. I shot *Slash*'s most vocal writer Claude "Kick Boy" Bessy, K.K. with his girlfriend Farrah Faucet-Minor, the Weirdos' Dix Denney, Cherie the Penguin, Tony the Tiger, Mick "Sten Gun" of the Skulls who helped Brendan create the Masque, and various others hanging out there.

It was in the kitchen of X's apartment that Farrah christened me "Jenny Lens." Between that and the many photos and small circle of friends, this apartment holds a very special place in my heart. I never shot next door at the infamous "Plunger Pit," where Trudie, Hellin, Mary Rat, Trixie, and visiting bands partied and crashed. I remember seeing my nude Captain Sensible hanging over their toilet though.

Slash magazine staffers rented Larchmont Hall, near Paramount Studios for their inaugural show on July 8, 1977, which featured the Zeros, the Dils, and the Weirdos. I was stunned to find a shot of Sire founder Seymour Stein standing in the hallway. Archivist David Jones told me Stein was interested in signing the Weirdos, but never followed up on it. We both wonder how that would have changed the L.A. punk scene: if someone had finally paid attention to our music and our vital, energetic, creative community.

Slash promoted Devo early and often, and threw their first party on July 22, 1977, when Devo came to L.A. to perform here for the first time. They publicly debuted at the Starwood, and these shots of them dressed as "spud" with trash-filled garbage bags, pantyhose, and knee pads are very rare. Mark Mothersbaugh attended the party as Booji Boy. These party photos perfectly encapsulate the mood and look of the times: Exene holding the *Slash* issue with Johnny Rotten on the cover, "Slash" written in magic marker on Pleasant's bleached jeans (no one bleached or distressed jeans then, usually people ironed on patches!), the Japanese transformer toy on her belt, Exene's mischievous smile, and Pleasant's genuine surprise. All my shots from this party are brimming with fun, images with seminal performers, writers, fans, and others laughing and dancing.

Richard Meltzer, the influential rock writer, backstage and the Dictators onstage at the Whisky, July, 1977. I had no idea Meltzer was so connected and influential. When I think about all the writers, managers, and others I met whom I should have worked with, I could scream, cry, or just shake my head in wonder. What was I thinking? I do know this: I didn't want this to become my career. I didn't want to take photos because it was my job. But I had such a difficult time being published, credited, or paid. I had no idea how to make this work without becoming part of what Joni Mitchell called the "star-making machinery."

Around that time, I went to diet doctors and obtained biphetamines, otherwise known as "black beauties." I'd take half of one, be up for three days, live in my darkroom, and then crash. One morning after such a session, I got a phone call from the guys behind Iggy's fan club in San Francisco. They were in Hollywood with Pleasant and Hellin, on their way to Iggy's rented beach house in Malibu, and wanted me to take photos. I told them my eyes were red, I was burned out, and I had no film. They picked me up and stopped at a drugstore on Sunset in the Palisades on the way.

Iggy painted on white paper that he cut from a large roll, then taped to the walls. I later heard these paintings were lost in storage, so perhaps I have the only

80

evidence of their existence. At one point he played a Cab Calloway album and I immediately perked up, being a huge fan of the man who wrote *Minnie the Moocher* and other songs in the early Betty Boop cartoons. Iggy saw my positive reaction, but puzzlingly played something else, bringing my energy level back down. One of the guys told me later that Iggy liked to play with people like that. I love Iggy; he can do no wrong. I have a shot of Iggy and me at the piano, playing and singing.

I love this shot of Alejandro (of the Nuns) and Javier (of the Zeros), the Escovedo brothers. I often hear or read that punk was white. Well, not on the West Coast. Los Angeles punks embraced all cultures, races, nationalities, and religions. Belinda in her often-referenced large trash-bag dress, with Terry "BagDad" Graham, drummer for the Bags and Gun Club. I love the shots contrasting typical 1970s fashions with my punk friends. No one dressed as they did. They didn't look to stylists nor the latest fashions. They picked up thrift store clothes for pennies, often wearing something once. Dressing the way we did often meant people swore or threw things at us. We were radical!

The second *Slash* magazine benefit took place on August 5, 1977, at Larchmont Hall. I took one of my favorite shots there: Mary Rat and Trudie Arguelles, with Hellin Killer in the background to left. They were among the most popular punkettes, all of whom also grew up in affluent beach cities. The could have looked like the average American beauty: blonde, tan, fuzzy pink sweater, and aviator glasses. Natasha in the Larchmont ladies room looks like a red-headed Betty Boop crossed with Lana Turner, so very sweet and stylish.

I still can't believe I wrangled an official photo pass to shoot Kiss during the recording of their landmark live double platinum album, *Kiss Alive II*. AC/DC debuted at the Whisky the next night and I spied a painted Iggy in the crowd, holding the paper parasol from my shots in his living room.

The Nuns opened for Chris Spedding and Bryan Ferry at Winterland on June 11, 1977. I totally forgot about my shot of Chris Spedding until Kimberly Bright inquired about my shots and used it for the cover of her biography of him. I love this shot for a million reasons, not least because he's one of the sexiest men ever to pick up a guitar. I had no idea of his history, and have photos of him with Robert Gordon and Link Wray. But who did I shoot all night? Chris. What did I know about Link Wray?

Jenny Lens and her punk pals Mary Rat and Hellin Killer, at Farrah's "She had to leave Los Angeles" farewell party on September 17, 1977. X and Black Randy debuted. I often wore Matisse- and Fauve-inspired makeup and tons of pins and jewelry. I couldn't afford clothes, but I loved to turn party favors and junk into jewelry to wear going out to shows or parties.

We went to Denny's on Hollywood Boulevard near the freeway after Farrah's party at 6th and Van Ness. Frustration, alienation, discrimination, and boredom on the faces of Tomata du Plenty, Hellin Killer, and Tony the Tiger. I remember Tomata telling me the wait staff at Denny's wouldn't seat them. I hadn't noticed because I don't eat after dark, had no money for food, and was having too much

fun taking great photos. Hellin, with her pencil-thin Jean Harlow eyebrows and LeSac bag, looks more vulnerable than anyone would believe, and Tony is clearly mad.

People often ask me if the police ever gave me a hard time. I wasn't part of the hardcore scene, but music professionals (writers and record company personnel, publicists and managers) often looked at me strangely. I'd be talking about the Ramones, X, or the Screamers, but they couldn't reconcile loving my shots with this wild woman. This shot perfectly captures the downside of our behavior and appearance. Pretty tame by today's standards, but we broke barriers, sometimes at great personal cost.

September 23, 1977, at the Tower Records press conference before the Punk Fashion Show at the Hollywood Palladium. My two good pals, exotic Alice Bag and Lobotomy founder, Pleasant Gehman, leaning against *the* 1970s

Eddie Van Halen, backstage at the Whisky, 1977.

car, a Volkswagen, across the street from my apartment. Hal Negro, Hellin Killer, Trudie, Pleasant, Darby Crash, Nickey Beat, Alice Bag, Delfina, Lorna Doom, Pat Smear and Jena Cardwell were a great lineup of people who were changing our culture, out for a day of fun, music, and mayhem. The Weirdos and Devo played, but I only wanted to shoot Blondie. But their manager grabbed my arm and literally dragged me out, leaving quite a bruise. He wouldn't believe that I had called for permission for the *Back Door Man* cover, even though I didn't even need it. He called me a liar, but Debbie was always very sweet to me. That incident caused decades of sorrow, and now it's on the cover of my first solo book. Who's smiling now?

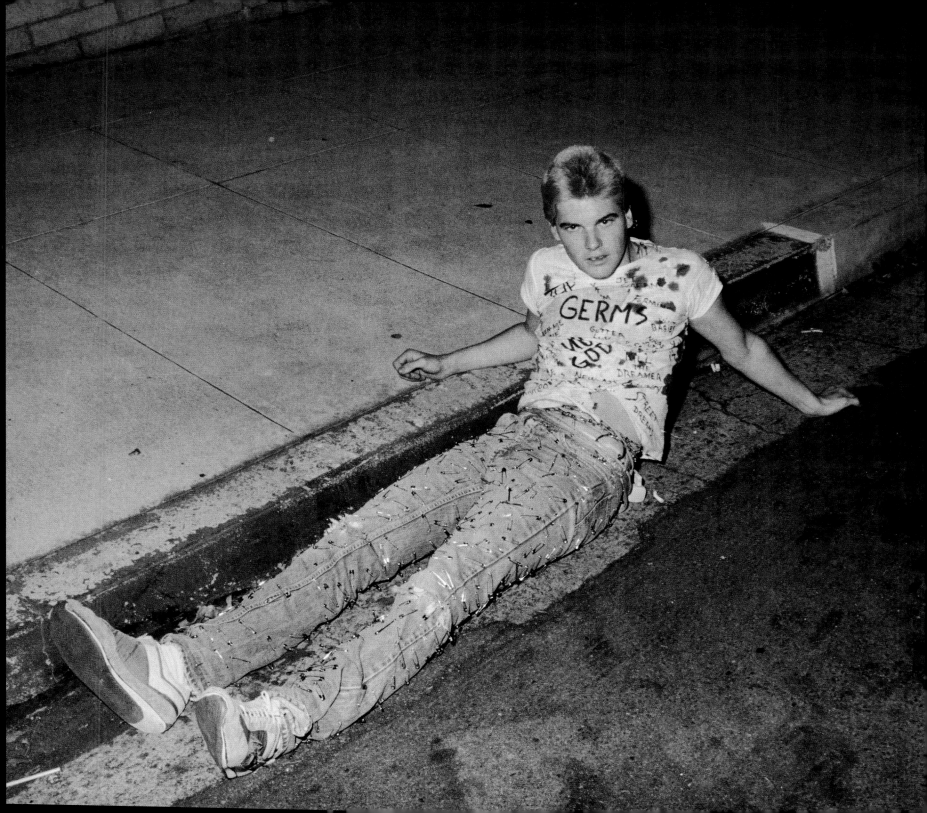

The Germs' first official photo shoot in June, 1977. Pleasant called me because she had convinced *Slash* magazine to publish her interview with them. This book's designer, Mark Martinez, joined us for a wild trek down Sunset Boulevard.

I chose Jenny for my first name because of several songs: "Jenny the Pirate" from *Threepenny Opera*, "Jenny Take a Ride" by Mitch Ryder and the Detroit Wheels, but initially when I heard Barbra Streisand's "Jenny Rebecca" when I was fourteen years old.

Barbra is a nice Jewish girl constantly being targeted because she is such a strong, independent, brilliantly talented, outspoken woman who literally does everything her way. What is more punk than that? She's an ideal honorary Germ at the Licorice Pizza, a record store across from the Whisky.

Previous pages: Lorna and Darby, 1977.

X's apartment: Joan Jett, Exene, Pleasant, Rand McNally (a.k.a. Pat Garrett), John Doe, and their typewriter.

The Weirdos and Zeros performed at the first *Slash* magazine benefit at Larchmont Hall, July 8, 1977. Seymour Stein, founder of Sire Records, at far left. Chase Holiday with Michael Romero choking Micol Sinatra (RIP) of the Extremes.

This *Slash* magazine benefit once raised seventy-seven dollars to publish an issue they would sell for fifty cents (when we didn't get them free or steal them). Left to right: Weirdos drummer Nicky Beat in fake leopard coat; the Germs' Darby Crash when he was still Bobby Pyn, wearing the same safety-pinned pants he wore in the gutter on Sunset Boulevard and wrestling with Pat Smear of the Germs and Nirvana; and the Runaways' Joan Jett and Lita Ford with Rodney Bingenheimer.

Pat Smear, Germs guitarist.

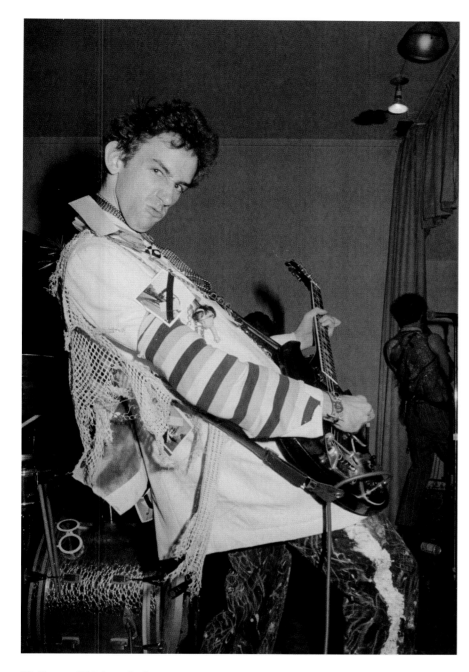

Dix Denney, Weirdos guitarist.

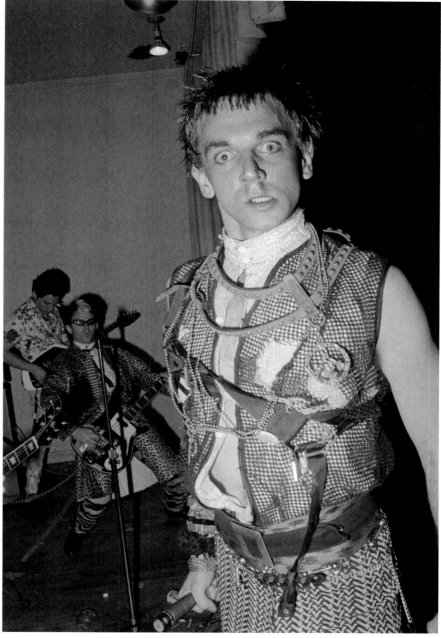

John Denney, lead singer of the Weirdos, with bassist Cliff Roman and guitarist Dave Trout behind him, July 8, 1977.

Devo as Spuds at the Starwood, August 22–24, 1977.

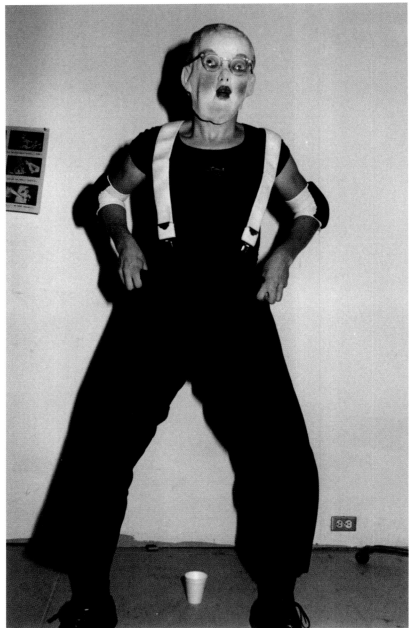

Booji Boy at the *Slash* Devo party, July 22, 1977.

Exene and Pleasant in the shower at the Devo party.

Following pages: Portraits of the artist as a young man. Iggy painting in his rented Malibu beach house, 1977.

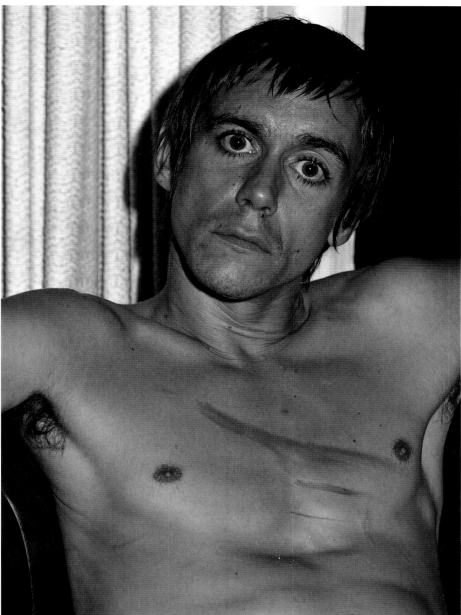

Escovedo brothers Alejandro of the Nuns and Javier of the Zeros, backstage at the Whisky in July 1977.

Future Go-Go Belinda in a trash bag dress with Terry Graham, drummer for the Bags and Gun Club, in August, 1977. I asked Terry what had inspired him to wrap black electrical tape over his pants and shoes and he merely shrugged his shoulders.

Drummer Terry "BagDad" Graham of Bags and Gun Club, Germs bassist Lorna Doom, future Go-Go Belinda, Hellin Killer, Cliff Hanger, and Pleasant. Just a typical night out. Nobody looked like they did. No budget, no stylists, just thrift stores and collaborations with one another.

Hellin Killer, Mary Rat, and Trudie Arguelles at the second *Slash* benefit, August 5, 1977.

Natasha as a punk Betty Boop meets Lana Turner, at the second *Slash* benefit, August 5, 1977.

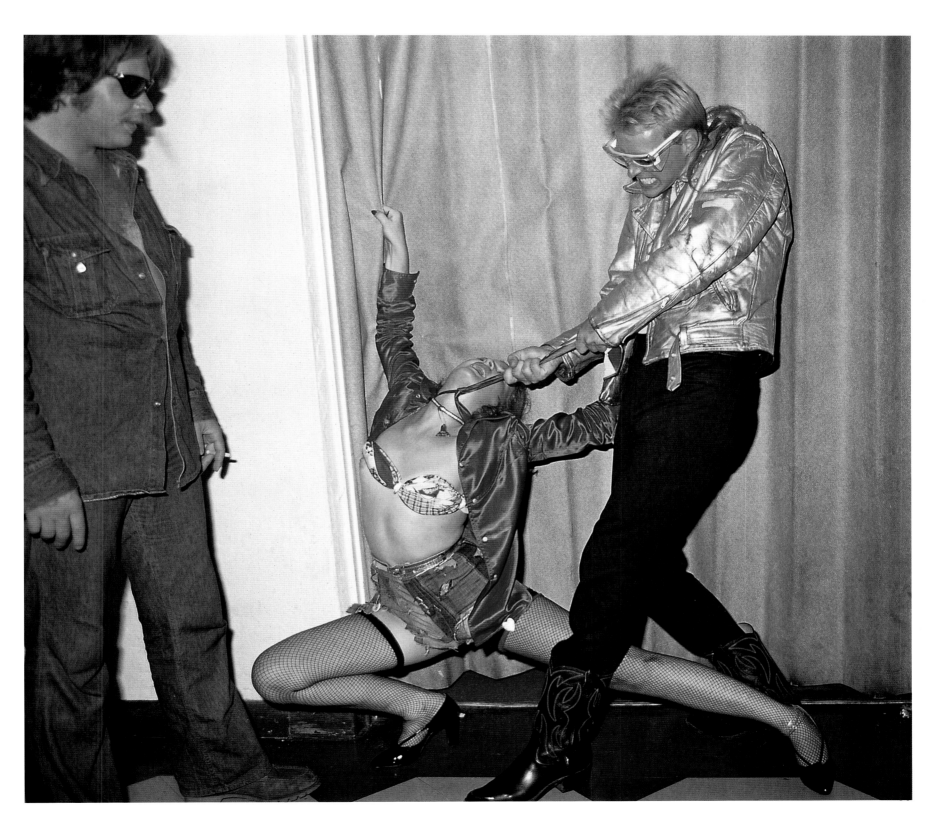

Alice Bag, Belinda, Hellin Killer, and Pleasant Gehman, August 21, 1977.

Previous pages: Tomata du Plenty, Tommy Gear, and Pleasant, August 21, 1977.

Top Jimmy, Pandora, and X's Billy Zoom, at the second Slash benefit, August 5, 1977.

Dueling guitarists Joan Jett and Lita Ford of the Runaways at the Whisky, August 26–27, 1977. This photo was published first in *Slash* and bootlegged later as a poster.

The Weirdos at the Whisky, summer, 1977.

Iggy painted his body before hanging out with Bon Scott when AC/DC made their L.A. debut at the Whisky, August 29–31, 1977.

Kiss at the L.A. Forum during the recording of their *Alive II* platinum classic, August 28, 1977.

Ric Ocasek of the Cars during the taping of *Midnight Special*, September 28, 1979.

Chris Spedding (swoon) played with Bryan Ferry. This photograph appears on the cover of Chris's recent biography. Mark Martinez and I were there in San Francisco that night, watching our favorite band, the Nuns, opening.

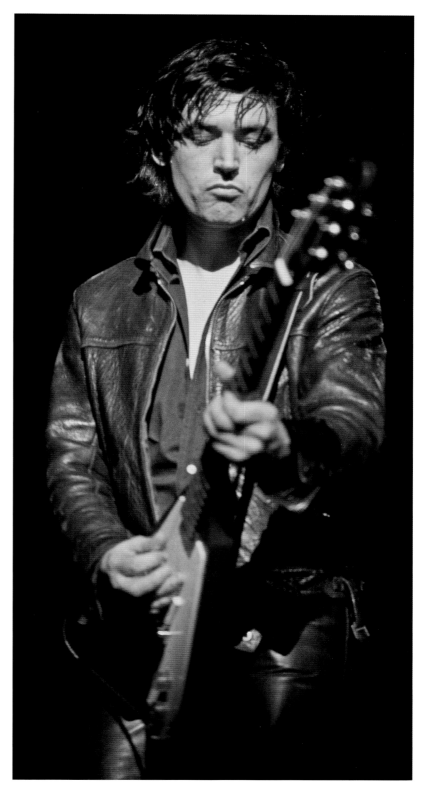

Mary Rat, Jenny Lens, and Hellin Killer at Farrah's good-bye party, September 17, 1977.

Band of Outsiders: Tomata du Plenty, Hellin Killer, and Tony the Tiger, not being seated at Denny's in Hollywood the same night, September, 1977.

Alice Bag and Pleasant Gehman, Tower Records parking lot,
September 23, 1977. We gathered for a disorganized press
conference prior to the "Uncle Punk Wants You! Punk Rock and
Fashion Show," with Blondie, the Weirdos, Devo, and Avengers
were at the Hollywood Palladium later that night.

Hal Negro, Hellin Killer, Trudie, Pleasant, Darby, Nickey Beat, Alice Bag, Delphina, Lorna Doom, Pat Smear, and Jena Cardwell.

The end of 1977 and the beginning of 1978 brought major changes. Our little L.A. punk scene was exploding. Many credit the Masque, a place for locals to play, practice, perform, and live. I was equally attracted to the Whisky and Starwood for hosting the New York, British, and San Francisco bands (and a few from Ohio). 1977 was truly our "favorite year." But great progress comes at a price. Authorities like the police, fire marshals, trendy posers, and kids out to get kicks by literally kicking began to infiltrate our little art and music scene. Life would never be as much fun and we'd never feel as free to be ourselves again.

Some say the implosion of the Sex Pistols proved that punk was not viable. Record companies poured so much money into disco and refused to take punk or new wave or power pop seriously. I've always said that the British and then the American press went crazy over a few words that Steve Jones uttered on the BBC. The media and record companies were just waiting for the right moment to pounce and make things even more difficult for bands like the Ramones, who were poised for radio and press acceptance and promotion. All eyes were on New York and British bands, and if they didn't succeed, why gamble on L.A.? That moment was grabbed away from us, because big business had too much to lose if the kids were really all right and did it for themselves.

The wisest question was asked by Johnny Rotten: "Ever get the feeling you've been cheated?" I will never forget hearing him ask us that. Yes indeed. But it comes with the territory — all pioneers are ridiculed and attacked. The first generation are not usually the ones who reap the benefits: fame, money, long careers. Only a few make it to the top, and usually they have great drive and ambition, good timing and some serendipity. But that's no reason not to rejoice in what we managed to accomplish.

Immediately after the Pistols fell apart, we returned to L.A. to find out that the Masque was being closed to the public. Bands performed at a landmark weekend Masque Benefit show in February, 1978, an amazing gathering of music, fashion and fun. Shows and parties continued to happen surreptitiously at the Masque, but only for those in the very inner circle. Brendan Mullen, the Masque's ringmaster, started to present shows around town. He found other sites, but nothing was quite like the first location. I have so many still-unpublished photos

of shows there, but I mostly went there for fun, to drink, and sometimes get laid. It was too hard for me to photograph, and once in a while I needed to be freed from my camera and go wild.

My dear friend Gaby Berlin reminded me of the time we found bottles of champagne in a bag near a parking lot by the Masque. She asked me how we did that and I replied, "Oh Gaby, you could find anything in that decrepit neighborhood." We each drank a bottle and got so wasted, which sounds like something I'd only do at the Masque. Gaby has told me she always had the most fun with me and was so sad I had to work in my darkroom so often. That's the trade-off: so many of my photos that helped promote and document the early punk scene were the result of not going to the Masque. One friend, Michael Romero (in the shot with Seymour Stein of Sire Records), called me all the time, usually after midnight. He'd yell at me to come to the Masque, and I'd tell him I was in my darkroom, a little walk-in closet. Gaby has shots of Michael trying to rip off my clothes. He was silly, but never meant any harm. Just another fun-loving crazy punk!

I often think about that period, more than any other times in punk. I worked so hard and gave up some fun times. My friends say I haven't changed — I still work more than I go out. I turn down invitations to rock and art shows, dinners, and parties all the time. I have all these amazing photos and stories to tell that no one else can tell the way I can tell them. I took the photos I wanted to take, I wasn't drunk, I have a great memory, and people constantly write or call and share their wonderful memories. As Mark and others say, I'm the historian, the storyteller. What would you do?

I caught a classic shot of Hellin Killer and her cat o'nine tails whip, with Pleasant and Darby dancing to Devo at the Starwood. Hellin copped her look from Su Catwoman, an early British Sex Pistols fan. Darby, still Bobby Pyn, was so young, blonde, and skinny. Pleasant and Darby had been friends for some time. Pleasant played a *huge* part in their success, with her *Slash* interview, coverage in her fanzine *Lobotomy*, helping them with their "look," and more. She's an unsung heroine in their story. The dog collars, the paper clip necklace, wearing 1950s cat-eye sunglasses indoors — all radical and innovative for their time. Mary Rat, Trudie, the Bags' Craig Lee (RIP), and children were dancing.

Stiv Bators, with a chain on his nipple, leaning backward with Cheetah Chrome during the Dead Boys' L.A. debut at Starwood on November 13, 1977. I've seen footage of these shows with Trudie, Hellin, and Mary at the foot of the stage, packed in like sardines. I have *no* idea how I took those — how did I get so close to the stage with no room to move? I have a shot of Trixie giving Stiv a blowjob while he's at the mic. He also shoved spaghetti down his pants, drooled beer down his chest — anything to be outrageous.

Iconic shots of Darby Crash singing with the Germs at the Masque, November 23, 1977. Bassist Lorna Doom and other female musicians playing loud, fast, angry music was a revolutionary act for that time. The Eyes with future Go-Go Charlotte, future X drummer DJ Bonebrake and Joe Nardini, all of whom soon became involved in other bands. The Eyes were unique because they spawned legendary bands, but also because this "lost" band was forceful, with dark songs and great energy. Imagine the Go-Gos' Charlotte screaming "She's dead!"

The Sex Pistols' last show at Winterland, January 14, 1978 (the Avengers and the Nuns opened). My most miserable memories. Squished into a VW, with Trudie on my lap in the front seat on the long drive, my flash damaged, standing in line for hours in the cold, damp air. Standing on a narrow photo box, constantly being knocked off, and shooting like crazy. Going backstage after the show. Being told by photographer Richard Creamer, "Jenny, you should have a photo pass." I was too shy, too sure I'd be turned down. How silly — I knew so many connected with the show, I was published, I was famous. But it was San Francisco, foreign terrain, and I thought Warner Brothers would say yes to people like Richard and no to me, so I didn't ask. I was sad Malcolm McLaren denied us Angelenos the opportunity to see the Pistols. I felt he cheated the band too. Look how we treated the Damned, the Ramones, Blondie — great venues, great parties, we earned it, they earned it. Yes, Johnny, you were right: we were *all* cheated.

After the show, I shot at San Francisco's famed punk club, the Mabuhay, when the Weirdos performed. Finally, I was at a party with Sid Vicious and Hellin Killer, who locked themselves in the bathroom. I discovered my flash didn't work, so I allowed Robbie "Posh Boy" Fields to seduce me. Gaby remembers my giggling all night as he chased me around until he finally caught me.

Steve Jones and Paul Cook came down to L.A. with the Avengers, who were managed by Rory Johnston, who worked for Malcolm McLaren. We all converged at the Masque, January 17, 1978. The Masque was closed to the public because of various fire and police violations.

Exene and her younger sister, Mirielle: "Riding with Mary," March 5, 1978. I took the last photos of Mirielle (Mary Kathryn) alive in 1980. I couldn't go to the X show the night of her death — although I looked forward to it, I had a strange sense of foreboding and couldn't bring myself to go. Notice the jewelry that Mirielle created. She had a clothing store in New York and one of her clients was Madonna, who became aware of the L.A. fashion scene and our habit of wearing lingerie in public thanks to Exene's sister and the early punk fanzines. Our thrift shop clothes would be worth a fortune today.

Poet and prophet David Byrne, Talking Heads debut, Whisky, December 15, 1977.

The Jam's debut at the Whisky, October 7, 1977.

Hellin Killer, Pleasant, and Bobby Pyn, a.k.a. Darby Crash, dancing to Devo with Mary Rat, Trudie, and Craig Lee of the Bags dancing behind them.

Following pages: The Ramones at the Whisky, 1977.

The Dead Boys' Stiv Bators and Cheetah Chrome on their Starwood debut, November 13, 1977.

Kim Fowley and Joan Jett, backstage at the Whisky during Runaways shows, December, 1977.

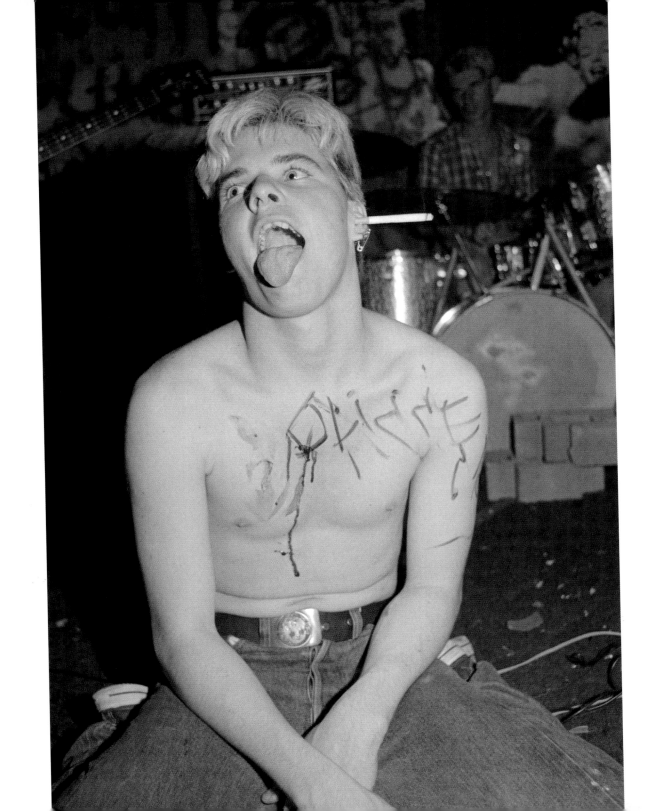

Germs Bassist Lorna Doom and future Gun Club founder and singer Jeffrey Lee Pierce sitting on the left. Nickey Beat on drums, temporarily a blonde. Nickey was the Weirdos' drummer, but also played with the Bags and other bands.

Opposite: The Eyes at the Masque with future Go-Go Charlotte yelling "She's dead!," future X drummer D.J. Bonebrake, and Joe Nardini.

Previous pages: Darby Crash of the Germs at the Masque, November 23, 1977.

Following pages: The Sex Pistols' last show at Winterland, and Paul Cook (Cookie) and Steve Jones (Jonesy) hanging out at the Mabuhay in San Francisco, January 14, 1978.

The last "official" night of the first Masque, January 17, 1978. Paul Cook of the Sex Pistols sitting at the Skulls' drum kit.

The Germs' Lorna Doom and Darby Crash, looking like two little tired and cold kids at the Masque, January 17, 1978.

Musician Chas Gray, who sound-proofed and helped to build the Masque with MC Bruce Barf. I love the turntables—back then we had no Walkmans, no iPods, nothing but records. January 17, 1978.

Avengers singer/songwriter Penelope Houston and drummer Danny Furious ascending the Masque stairs. This shot was attributed to another photographer in a *Live at the Masque* CD booklet. The lack of another staircase was the main reason the Masque was forcibly closed on January 17, 1978.

A rare shot of the mythic Randoms: Dangerhouse Records' Rand McNally and drummer KK Barrett, also of the Screamers, Oklahoma friends and X's John Doe. This might be the only photo of them at the Masque, January 17, 1978.

Opposite: My favorite shot of one of my all-time favorites: the voice of Slash, charismatic and charming, the beloved Claude "Kick Boy" Bessy (RIP). Also lead singer of Catholic Discipline, he can be seen in *Decline of Western Civilization*. At the Masque, January 17, 1978.

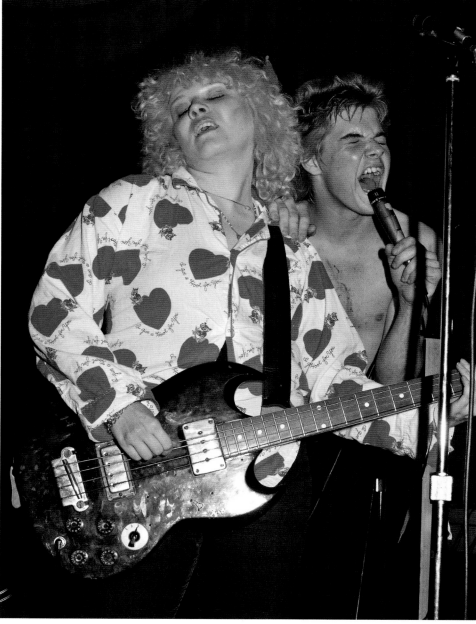

Fiery, stylish Penelope Houston, the Avengers lead singer/songwriter, at the Whisky on February 14–15, 1978.

The Germs' Lorna Doom and Darby Crash at the Masque Benefit at Elk's Lodge, MacArthur Park, February 24, 1978.

Opposite: Paul Collins of the Nerves, David Moon (the Ramones' first live L.A. Pinhead), and Trudie selling tickets, and Trixie and Donnie Rose (RIP) at the Masque benefit, February 25, 1978.

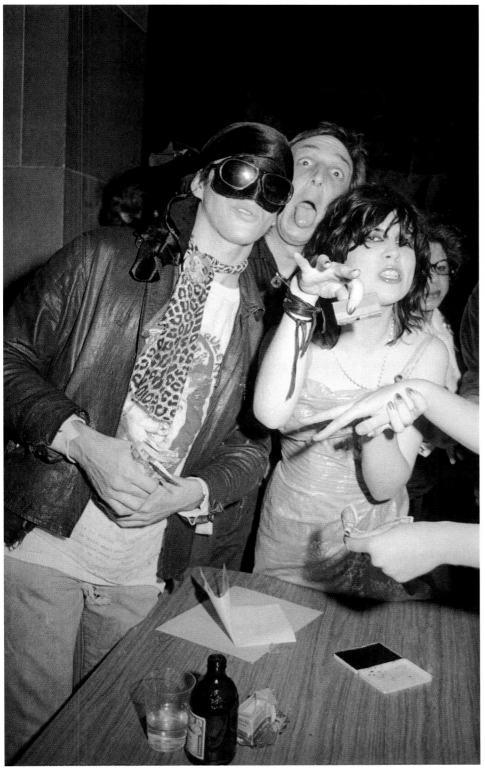

Alice Bag holding Elvis Presley in his *Jailhouse Rock* clothes.

Alice, like Elvis, broke many barriers, including being a Latina in punk. Many say Alice, as much as Darby, was the original hardcore punk singer. Off stage, she's a wonderful friend, loving mother and wife, award-winning teacher, profoundly intelligent and sensitive writer, and a talented visual artist with a beautiful voice and soul.

Alice and I never bought into believing we are defined by our upbringing or cultural backgrounds. Life changes, people change, and the more you embrace the chance to reinvent yourself and adapt to changes around you, the more fully you can participate in a joyful, meaningful life.

Change is growth. Fear of change is death. That's what set L.A. punks apart from so many others: we were open to changes, exploration, trying something new. That meant creating new communities, families, relationships, and new traditions that might alienate others. The shock of the new.

Beloved L.A. punk band the Bags, February 24, 1978: Mark Moreland, Patricia Morrison, Alice Bag, and Craig Lee, with temporary drummer and Alice's boyfriend Nickey Beat. Screamer K.K. Barrett is on the side.

X at the Masque benefit, February 25, 1978, with John Doe, Exene in a rhinestone thrift-shop tiara, Billy Zoom minus his ubiquitous silver leather jacket, with drummer D.J. making his X public debut.

Opposite: Black Randy: Angel or Devil? His Randettes, a take-off of Ike and Tina Turner's Ikettes, were rotating members of the L.A. punk scene.

Future producer and Masque fixture Geza X with Spaz Attack in "Arthur J and the Gold Cups," a Masque Production at the Whisky, March 5, 1978.

The Dickies appeared on NBC's *CPO Sharkley* starring Don Rickles on March 7, 1978. Trixie, Kid Congo, Alice Bag, Spaz Attack, and Mary Rat were punk "extras." The Dickies included drummer Carlos Caballero, guitarist Stan Lee, singer Leonard Philips (with his Wolfman hand), and Billy Club in the rear. Missing in this shot is Chuck Wagon, who later killed himself.

Previous pages: Exene and her sister Mireille visiting from New York. The Masque presented Black Randy and the Metrosquad at the Whisky on March 5, 1978. Trudie, Sheila Edwards, Trixie, Connie Clarksville, Alice Bag, Spaz Attack, Nickey Beat, and K.K. Barrett gathered for a quick shot.

Johnny Rotten and Joan Jett, with Joan's friend Lisa Curland in the mirror, at the Whisky on March 9, 1978. This is an infamous shot, often bootlegged, and apparently it even appears on a picture disk I haven't seen.

St. Patrick's Day, March 17, 1978, Pleasant's birthday party at the fabled Tropicana Motor Hotel, hotel and home of many musicians, including Marianne Faithfull and photographer Leee Black Childers. I wanted to take more photos of Marianne, but due to her being high, I wouldn't. It was such a thrill after "as time goes by" to be face-to-face with such a 60s icon.

Arthur Lee (RIP) at the Starwood, with surprise guest Patti Smith on May 3, 1978. Arthur was the late singer of Love, a revered L.A. 60s band. My dear friend Rosemarie Patronette told me she and her close friend, Velvert Turner (RIP), pretended to be Patti and Arthur. They called and told each other to meet up at the show. I was thrilled to dance with Patti.

One of the joys of delving into my archive is digging up little gems, but figuring our who, what, where, and when is so time-consuming. Roger Gastman asked me if I had shots of the Screamers at the Stardust Ballroom for potential inclusion in his *Live at the Masque* tome (he used thirty-three of my shots, but only "Crime" from this show). I often pondered where I shot some color images of Tommy Gear against a white curtain. I shot the Dils and DOA at that site, but didn't connect the backdrop to the Screamers until we spoke. Then I zoomed in to take a better look and saw a fuzzy blonde head at the corner of the stage, in a black dress. I realized that it was Chase. In 2007 I met Megan Dymond at a DVD presentation I created with dozens of my Screamers shots. She kept insisting that she was in my photos, so I invited her over and was delighted when she identified herself in one of my all-time favorite color shots, with Chase and Alice Bag.

I flew to Houston at 2 a.m. to photograph the Stones and Peter Tosh the day before my 28th birthday on July 19, 1978. I knew I couldn't get a photo pass to shoot them at Anaheim Stadium in Orange County, which held 60,000 — larger than any L.A. venue. I shot them in the smaller Sam Houston Auditorium, Texas, the most hot and humid show I ever photographed. I met the lighting man afterwards, who admitted he didn't light Keith Richards properly. Can you imagine not lighting *both* the Glimmer Twins? Mick Jagger wore a souvenir Texas T-shirt and his fingernails were painted green. My photos appeared in Japanese magazines and on 45 singles for the *Coming Home* soundtrack.

Bob Marley at the Starlight Amphitheater, July 22, 1978, and Peter Tosh, backstage on an unicycle and opening for the Stones, at the Anaheim Stadium, July 23, 1978. I snuck between two big burly guards to run backstage to see Marley, but my new Nikon camera didn't work correctly. I shot a whole roll of Bob and Peter Tosh, but the film didn't advance. By the time I realized what the problem was, Peter had left. I believe it was the last time those two were publicly together.

In 1976 I went to Anaheim Stadium and used binoculars to see the Who, Aerosmith, and others, never dreaming I'd ever stand on that stage and take photos. I love this shot of Peter because he's so self-contained, dancing and facing me, and I could include a few of the 60,000 in attendance. I still am incredulous that I was on that stage taking photos.

Punk, like life, doesn't always run a straight course or tie together. I tried to cover as much music, art, and old movies as I could, while working so hard to be published. This scene defies easy compartmentalization because L.A. punks were not easy to define. Like our city, we covered a wide terrain. I deliberately avoided the outdoor daytime skateboarders. I love to swim, but kneel next to an empty pool in the bright sunlight? I don't tan, I burn. I wear sandals, so hardcore shows held no appeal for me.

Otherwise I devoured a wide range of music, as did my friends in so many photos. Devo, Warhol, the Germs, rockabilly, disco, and a pioneering female performer and producer and DJ: just a few typical nights out on the town. I'm in the video of Devo taping "Come Back Jonee" at the Roxy on September 28, 1978, wearing a flowered dress, having come straight from a record company event. Devo fans love this Bob Mothersbaugh shot. Warhol and the late Divine visited Fiorucci's on September 22, 1978 — I couldn't believe it, I was just inches from Warhol, though of course I was too shy to speak to him.

Darby Crash, the Germs' lead singer, and Hellin Killer, around December 1978 He wore same white jacket at the Roxy during the filming of the Ramones' *Rock 'n' Roll High School*. I recall Darby saying, "Hey Jenny, take a look at this." Then Hellin removed his bandage. How and why did he have stitches all across his throat? It reminded me of Frankenstein. An early suicide attempt? I was so shocked, but I didn't feel comfortable asking him what had happened.

Marianne Faithfull and photographer/manager Leee Black Childers at a St. Patrick's Day birthday party for Pleasant Gehman at the Tropicana, March 17, 1978. Brendan Mullen in his office at the Masque.

The British Levi and the Rockats set L.A. ablaze with their hot sets and cool dudes. They, along with Ray Campi and the Rockabilly Rebels, whet our appetite for rockabilly and were precursors and mentors to the Stray Cats. They played the Whisky throughout 1978–1979, so it's hard to date this precisely. Stand-up bassist Smutty Smith was one of the *first* to sport tats (a lot of them). He also stood atop and cradled his bass and was quite the heartthrob.

Donna Summer, at the height of her fame as the Disco Queen and international star, joined her friend, Genya Raven, an unsung heroine in punk's early days. Genya's considerable talents affected many performers, not least producing the Dead Boys. L.A. punk fans neglected her at her shows at the Whisky on August 11–12, 1978. This is a major shot, comparable in its time to a shot of Madonna at the height of her career, appearing on stage in a tiny venue.

The most beautifully lit and emotionally poetic show I ever shot or saw was the Boomtown Rats, with future humanitarian Sir Bob Geldof, at the legendary Cocoanut Grove on March 2, 1979. The crumbling, decrepit club was the former glamour hot-spot during Hollywood's glory days. Movie stars ate, drank, and danced the nights away after working in the studios during the day.

The Rats never achieved the acclaim they deserved. They were wonderful to hang with (I have so many fun off-stage shots). Bob, accompanied only by pianist Johnny Fingers, debuted a song inspired by a news item, "I Don't Like Mondays." Now elaborately performed with strings and an orchestra, it lacks the punch, the intimate and emotional wallop I felt that night. Its simplicity and delivery, its melody, and Bob's brilliant perception that this incident — a young student, a female no less, shot at her school for no discernable nor easily stated reason — was not only a new phenomenon but a lasting one, and is but one example of the social awareness of this music called punk. Fatchna O'Kelley, their manager, gave me an advanced pressing with a sweet note, thanking me for my support.

The day the music died: a St. Patrick's Day punk show at the Elk's Lodge was interrupted by local L.A.P.D. I didn't go, but the police arrived in force, beating punks sitting on the stairs, watching the bands, or trying to flee the scene. No one knows who called the police or why. We gathered at the Masque the next day, March 18, 1979 for a press conference. The younger kids drank and fooled around, but the older ones realized dark days were on the horizon. Exene's eyes say it all: our days of freedom were over. It was incomprehensible to those in attendance why the police attacked the kids who were peaceably attending a legitimate show, with bands like the Go-Go's scheduled to play.

Exene was constantly accused of copying Siouxsie (of the Banshees). She's wearing a button of Siouxsie on her jacket. However, Exene, like myself, was far more influenced by silent film stars like the first "vamp," the first filmed Cleopatra, Theda Bara, born Theodosa Goodman — a nice Jewish girl from Chicago.

I saw the Police at Madame Wong's on May 18, 1979. I was never a Police fan, but I read all the British papers and I knew they were going to be huge. I arrived four hours before show time and sat at Sting's feet. Why was he eating a watermelon on stage?

The Boomtown Rats loved playing at unusual places. They performed at Frederick's of Hollywood, April 4, 1979. Before Victoria's Secret, Hustler, and the internet, the best place to buy racy lingerie was Frederick's. Adult toys and racy, decadent nights, when these pleasures were still so taboo and difficult to access.

A rare sighting: punks in eveningwear during the daytime, at Wattles Park on May 28, 1979. It was both Tomata du Plenty's and Liara's birthdays. Someone came to the park with their pet bird and this photo perfectly captures that moment. The image captures people in the prime of their lives — the beautiful yet troubled Liara would later overdose in a laundromat, and Tomata would succumb to cancer and AIDS.

On May 12, 1979, I photographed Blondie appearing on *American Bandstand*. Debbie told me I could shoot the dress rehearsal, but that their manager would be around for the taping. She knew he would throw me out, so she warned me not to try to shoot then. I grabbed this one quick shot, and it's much more interesting than anything we'd have seen on television. I love the casualness and the men working on the side while Dick gets to know Debbie. Dick Clark is a perfectly charming man, too.

Chuck Berry's trademarked duck walk at the Roxy, August 3, 1979. I licensed this to the William Morris Agency and it was used throughout the 1980s in various advertisements and posters. I was so thrilled to shoot four of his shows in such a small venue. While many cite Elvis Presley as their introduction to rock, for me it was always Chuck Berry and, to some degree, Little Richard. It's no coincidence the Beatles covered "Roll Over Beethoven" on their first album. We all owe a huge debt to Chuck Berry. I met him and his daughter Ingrid backstage. He was so kind to me, so humble and so willing to pose. I could never imagine, as a lonely kid singing and dancing along to his songs, that I would ever meet him or that my photo would become such an important part of his legacy.

June 19, 1979 (my mother's birthday) and I was about to drive away from the self-service gas station on Robertson and Olympic in Beverly Hills when I saw Bob Dylan in his car. He gave me a hard time about taking photos, but I got a few. I sent them to *Rolling Stone* and was woken very early by Kurt Loder calling from New York. I had no idea who he was, but I knew he was going far. No one ever contacted me for stories and I never forgot that call. Dylan was never important in my life. I know that's going to shock some, but I don't "get" him. He was so rude to me, I should have shot him pumping gas, but the nice Jewish girl in me held back.

I attended the Grammy ceremony in 1979, when Dylan won for best male vocal. I chased after someone and said that Elvis Costello was more deserving than Dylan. Brad Elterman, another photographer, asked me if I knew who that man was. Yes, I knew it was Dylan's manager, the very powerful Jerry Weintraub. But neither *Armed Forces* nor "Oliver's Army" were nominated, although they are still his most popular works. "Oliver's Army is a timeless classic." Elvis wanted to call the album "Emotional Fascism," a prescient description of our times.

To celebrate my twenty-ninth birthday on July 20, 1979, I dropped mushrooms. I love and miss hallucinogens. I remember not being able to focus because I was hallucinating so wildly. I almost threw out the film, but I loved the Screamers so much I figured it was worth the money to develop it. I printed a couple of shots that immediately grabbed my attention, then didn't look at the rest of the negatives for nearly twenty-seven years.

When I finally did scan and examine my negatives, this Screamers shot took my breath away. The shot is pure drama — look at both Tomata's and Sheila's intense expressions. I love the photographic quality, the soft drop shadow behind Tomata, and the soft focus of K.K. and Tommy. I cherish photos and film quality from the silent film era, which are different from the brilliant Technicolor films of the late 1930s through the 1940s, and the creative use of minimal light in film noir. I've studied so many stills and so many movies that still astound and delight me. That's what I felt finding this and other photos from this show. I've never seen anyone embody Edvard Munch's *The Scream* the way they both do here. It wasn't the ubiquitous pop culture icon it is today. Only art students and the cultured elite knew of the painting.

X at the Stardust Ballroom, New Wave 1980, August 30, 1979. How do I love this photo? Let me count the ways. The steam heat from John and Exene's sweaty bodies, the three swooning men at Exene's feet, the man dancing in the rear center, looking so much like the Circle Jerks' iconic image, and a dear friend of mine, in his red bandana, the talented Mark Vallen. Mark volunteered at *Slash* magazine, created memorable covers, and designed graphics for Penelope Spheeris' *Decline of Western Civilization*. I'm in that movie, swooning, just like the men in this photo. X had that effect on many of us.

A punk wedding on August 31, 1979 at Fiorucci's, a fabulous store on Rodeo Drive in Beverly Hills staffed with fashionable punks. Employees Marisol and LeRoy were married in the store. I can see the 1980s *Miami Vice* styles being born

Patti Smith and Arthur Lee (RIP) at the Starwood, May 3, 1978. Patti dancing with Rodney Bingenheimer, the Mayor of Sunset Boulevard —
Rodney DJ'd punk songs in another room at the Starwood, one of the few places you could dance to punk records.

here. I met Sham 69 and the Orchids, another Kim Fowley band, on September 7, 1979. Two days later I drove Sham around town, from Hollywood to Pasadena to their flight out at LAX.

Sham 69 were wonderful, but doomed because British skinheads adopted them. I drove them around in my blue Chrysler New Yorker, which Dee Dee Ramone loved. Bebe Buell, who was dating Elvis Costello was so sweet to me and told me to have more self-confidence. (She is also Liv Tyler's mother). I miss her loud-mouthed, abrasive pal, the late Michelle Myer, Whisky booker. Cramp Lux and Ivy also showed up for the Rodney on the ROQ radio show. Imagine half a roll of film of Sham 69, the other half full of shots taken at the Old Waldorf in San Francisco, November 26–29, 1979, with Iggy, Glen Matlock (the Sex Pistols' original bassist), Ivan Kral (keyboardist, guitarist, and songwriter who contributed so much to Patti's "Horses," the record that changed my life), Damned guitarist Brian James, and drummer Klaus Kruger.

The Bags were also performing in San Francisco and singer Alice Bag and bassist Patricia Morrison chatted with Glen. Patricia formed the early Goth band the Sisters of Mercy in England, married and has a daughter with Dave Vanian of the Damned. So the Bags "don't need the English?"

In September 1979 I shot Gang of Four. I love Gang of Four, but that always surprises people. Why can't I love the Clash and Gang of Four? I love the way Gang of Four bassist Dave Allen is looking at Stiv Bators, and members of Levi and the Rockats, precursors to the Stray Cats, blonde Dibble and the tattooed Smutty Smith.

The Germs played the Culver City Auditorium in December, 1979. People have the misconception that every Germs show was riotous, with a vigorous mosh pit and bedlam. Ron Reyes, a Black Flag singer, in the forefront, and another fan, are in deep reverie, hands on their foreheads. You can see Black Flag and SST Records founder Greg Ginn towards the back, Bill Bartell of White Flag near the stage, and many from *Flipside* magazine and the burgeoning South Bay/Orange County scene, which would soon dominate hardcore punk. Germs guitarist Pat Smear saw some of my slides and said I shot "Darby's Boys," including the late Donnie Rose, the too-long incarcerated Regi Mental, the late Dennis Darnell of Social Distortion, and the recently departed and dearly missed Tony the Tiger, all hanging around behind the band and clearly visible onstage.

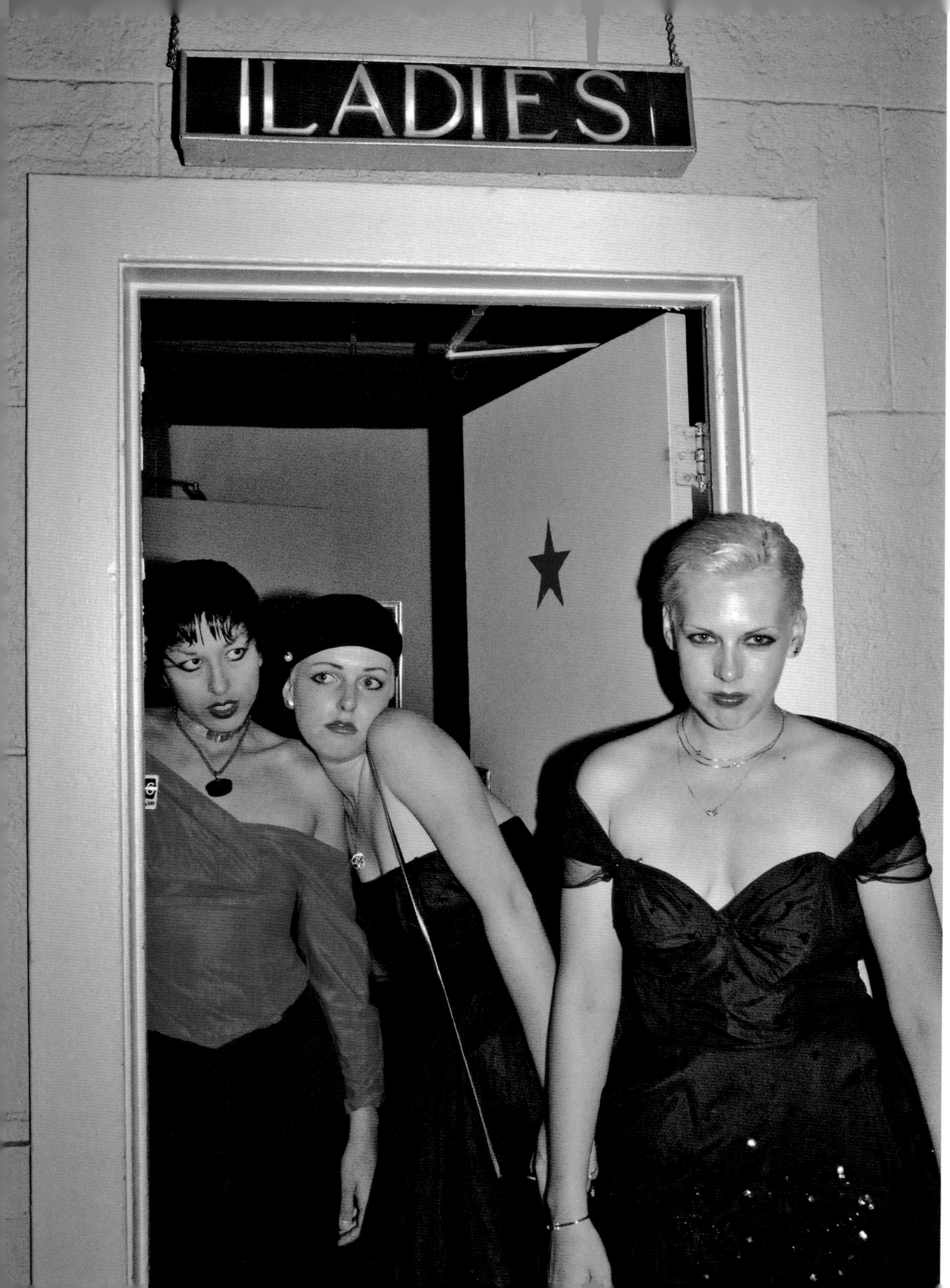
LADIES

Tom Waits and Trixie at Tropicana, summer of 1978.

Opposite: Alice Bag, Megan Dymond, and Chase Holiday at the Stardust Ballroom, July 3, 1978.

Following pages: The Rolling Stones and Peter Tosh at the Sam Houston Auditorium, Texas, July 19, 1978.

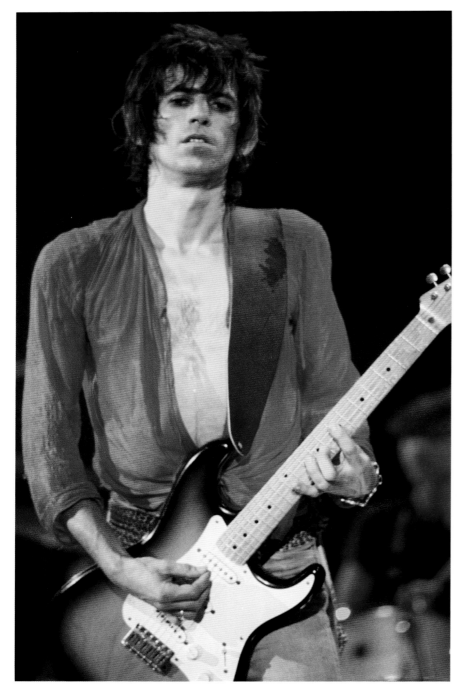

Peter Tosh, backstage on a unicycle and dancing in front of 60,000 at the Anaheim Stadium, opening for the Stones on July 23, 1978.

Opposite: Bob Marley backstage at the Starlight Amphitheater, July 22, 1978.

The Boomtown Rats, led by (not yet Sir) Bob Geldof, at the Coconut Grove, March 2, 1978.

Previous pages (clockwise from left): Devo Bob Mothersbaugh, circa 1978; Devo taping "Come Back Jonee" at the Roxy, September 28, 1978; Darby Crash of the Germs and Hellin Killer; Levi and the Rockats at the Whisky, circa 1978; Dead Boys producer Genya Raven joined by disco queen Donna Summer at the Whisky, August 11–12, 1978; and Andy Warhol at the Fiorucci's Beverly Hills opening on September 22, 1978.

Donnie Rose (RIP) and Gary Ryan (later the bassist with Joan Jett's Blackhearts and Lorna Doom's husband), with F-Word's lead singer/songwriter Rik L Rik (RIP), drinking from a paper bag while underage at a Masque press conference on March 18, 1979.

Opposite: Exene's eyes say it all: a darkness had descended upon punk. Exene created the poster for the St. Patrick's Day punk gala at the Elk's Lodge near MacArthur Park.

Hellin Killer and Darby Crash during the press conference.

The Boomtown Rats at Frederick's of Hollywood, April 4, 1979. They were so much fun!

Opposite: The Police — and Sting eating a watermelon onstage — at Madame Wong's in Chinatown, L.A., May 18, 1979.

Following pages: Birthday party for Liara and Tomata du Plenty, with Chase Holiday and wild bird at Wattles Park in West Hollywood, May 28, 1979.

Blondie's *American Bandstand* debut, performing Heart of Glass on May 12, 1979.

Chuck Berry and Little Richard were my early rock gods. Chuck was very gracious backstage at the Roxy on August 3, 1979.

Dylan got angry when I saw him filling his car on June 19, 1979.

was passionately devoted to the Screamers and X. It doesn't get any better than these two — summer, 1979.

Following pages: Punk wedding at Fiorucci's, August 31, 1979. Pre-*Miami Vice* style was closing in on punk.

Howard Devoto and Magazine, during their L.A. debut at the Whisky on August 30, 1979.

Sham 69 on top of my car and Jimmy Pursey in the hallway at KROQ.

The Cramps' Ivy and Lux with Sham 69, Rodney Bingenheimer, Bebe Buell, and Michelle Myers (RIP), a former Whiskey booker, at *Rodney on the ROQ* on September 9, 1979.

Iggy Pop and Glen Matlock, the original Sex Pistols bassist, at the Old Waldorf in San Francisco, November 29, 1979.

Opposite: Glen Matlock with Alice and Patricia Bag at the Old Waldorf in San Francisco.

Jon King, Hugo Burnham, and Dave Allen of Gang of Four, with Stiv Bators and Dibble and Smutty Smith of Levi and the Rockats, September, 1979.

Sham 69 at the Whisky, December 7, 1979.

The Germs at Culver City Auditorium in December, 1979. I love seeing the dudes swooning — Ron Reyes, one-time Black Flag singer, plus Greg Ginn (also of Black Flag), Bill Bartell, Dennis Danell (of Social Distortion), and many South Bay and hardcore fans.

New Year's, 1980, and X signed to Slash Records atop their Beverly Boulevard offices in West Hollywood. "We set the trash on fire." X and their pals, a.k.a. the Wolves, celebrated with *Slash*'s Bob Biggs, their attorney and manager Jay Jenkins, and as always Top Jimmy (RIP).

The shot of the Go-Go's at Starwood, in January, 1980, spontaneously captures their personalities: poised Jane, smiling Gina, reserved Charlotte, always laughing, co-founder and original bassist Margot, and hesitant Belinda, with both Jane and Belinda crossing their arms and framing the image. I knew them as party girls, the girls dancing next to me, the ones I loved to photograph — fun, but by now starting to become more serious about their music. I told Jane to start saving receipts, for things like guitar strings, and she thought I was out of my mind. Why should she have to worry about tax deductions?

The Valentine's Surreal Party, February 14, 1980, at the Wilton Hilton. Tommy and Tomata moved out, so this was my last Screamers party. I have amazing shots, everyone so creatively made up for the holiday, the house decorated imaginatively on so little money, as usual. I had a new Polaroid camera and captured a few shots of my last L.A. punk party of that era. There was a music room, and I have beautiful color slides of punks playing exotic instruments. We had fun, but the scene was changing. People were scattering in different directions, some to hang on and propel punk into hardcore dominance, or roots rock, or power pop, or take their message on the road, like the Go-Go's or X. Or break up, like the Screamers.

A rare color shot of the Hong Kong Café in the heart of L.A.'s Chinatown, March, 1980. High on acid, I danced while in line, right outside of Madame Wong's door, loudly singing X songs. Madame Wong was *not* into punk, especially punk women, who she felt "were trouble." The Hong Kong upstairs was a great venue for many struggling bands and didn't oppose loud, rowdy, hardcore punk groups. I will never forget how difficult it was to take photos that night, because it was so crowded. I stood next to huge amps beside John Doe and Exene, wearing her ever-present white bone bangles. I loved Top Jimmy and always thought of him at the fifth X member. After that show, Exene told me that she didn't know "any other photographer who could be high on acid, dance all night, and take so many great photos." A rare compliment!

I was on stage for the Clash at the Santa Monica Civic Auditorium on March 3, 1980, as cameras were forbidden on the floor. They were the best live band ever (and they didn't need fancy videos or big stages to explode in front of us), and that was one of the best Clash shows I ever shot. I stupidly told my neighbors the name and location of the black-and-white lab. They broke into it and stole my negatives. They had to be the most amazing shots I ever took of the Clash, gone forever.

They were the most amazing band, bar none. I had so much access to them in L.A., San Francisco, and England, but I never spoke to them or shot them offstage, other than a quick casual shot. I was so shy and intimidated by them. I developed intimate relationships with various members of their road crew. But I didn't go after them, and I never took advantage of such close access. It was like standing too close to the sun: I just melted around the Clash.

In the spring of 1980, X filmed *Decline of Western Civilization* at West L.A.'s Club 88, a little working-class bar on Pico that was receptive to various punk shows. Although the film is a major distortion of the scene — it's very subjective, focusing on the more nihilistic, destructive aspects of L.A. punk rather than its more artistic and thoughtful participants — I have to thank Penelope for capturing X on film.

I attended X's BBQ at their Genesee apartment, around the corner from the X-rated Pussycat Theater on Santa Monica Boulevard. I walked outside and saw Exene and the golden late afternoon sunlight. I asked her to pose with the motorcycles and the sun illuminated her face so beautifully. My favorite time of day is sunset, but I rarely had the opportunity to shoot outdoors. Her name is on one of the bikes, but I don't know if it was hers or just an homage to her.

Top Jimmy was always feeding people. I have a cute color shot of Jimmy cooking with Belinda, another with Tomata and members of the Dickies and the Quick. This shot reveals the close friendship between X and the Go-Go's. Billy Zoom, Charlotte, Gina, Jane, original bassist and co-founder Margot, and John Doe. The camera didn't forward the film correctly, but the photograph is precious for their expressions and the knowledge this little community was soon to spread out and these kinds of intimate events would radically change, with new faces replacing some of the familiar ones.

The Go-Go's at the crossroad, March 8, 1980. Mark Martinez designed their logo, which you can partially see on the drum. He still has the original drawing. This was 1960s pop colliding with 1970s punk, leading the way to the 1980s. After countless performances in which they were too nervous even to move on stage, they got it together. Even their clothes anticipate 1980s fashions, with Charlotte's 1960s holdout of the black-and-white mini-dress. I was saving money and about to buy a video camera to shoot them before their first English trip, but the day after I took the money out of the bank I was robbed at gunpoint.

Exene and John married April 6, 1980, on Easter Sunday in Tijuana. We all celebrated the release of *Los Angeles* from Slash Records, produced by the Doors' Ray Manzarek, at the Whisky, April 11. Exene's younger sister Mary, a.k.a. Mirielle, starred in *Ecstatic Stigmatic*, a short film directed by her husband Gordon about a young woman in the 1930s celebrated for her stigmata. They visited from New York to show the film at the Pan Andreas Theatre on April 14 and 15 and to celebrate X's success.

I shot the band, minus drummer D.J. Bonebrake, but with Ray. I took color and black-and-white shots of Exene's lovely sister. The next night I stayed home and shot heroin. I don't know why, I hated it. X was my favorite band, why would I miss that show? I just knew I couldn't go. Claude "Kick Boy" Bessy visited me the following morning. He, like everyone, knew how much I loved X. Exene had raised her younger sister after their mother died from cancer. Mirielle was killed on her way to the show in a newly purchased used car driven by Farrah, the subject of the song "Los Angeles."

Claude was so kind, so concerned about how I would take the news and wanted to tell me personally. X played the Hollywood Palladium a few days after returning from the Florida funeral. I hated shooting there because it was impossible to get good shots. Exene wore her sister's Dodger jacket and I caught a glimpse of her grief. I never drive without a little statue of the Virgin Mary, "protection to pass."

I love the shot of Top Jimmy and Exene, with the apricot roses the Whisky gave X to honor their new album. This shot perfectly captures their friendship and Jimmy's warm, engaging, bluesy personality. Top Jimmy worked at Top Taco on La Brea, across the street from A & M Records, formerly Charlie Chaplin's studio and currently Henson Productions. Jimmy fed punks for years and told a group of us that the elderly owners knew about it. Jimmy pointed to his forearm and said they were tattooed with numbers. Many didn't know the significance of being tattooed with numbers during World War II. I knew it meant they had survived the "concentration camps," a more acceptable euphemism for "extermination camps," and were Holocaust survivors. They knew what it was like to starve and they kept many punks alive.

Jimmy and Billy Zoom had been friends forever and Jimmy was our soulful storyteller, with a cig in his hand, a beer in front of him, that generous sexy grin and twinkling blue eyes. I have photos from that night of John and Exene giving Jimmy a tattoo with a ball and chain and a big "X." I loved being around him, such

a rare, good masculine man. His charm endeared everyone to him, no matter how drunk he became. He succumbed too early from too much drinking. I wish he were around to enjoy all this.

I raised as much money as I could and flew to England in June 1980 to see my two favorite bands: X and the Clash. After an eleven-hour flight, I picked up maps at Heathrow, found my way on the underground to a British rock paper's office, and dumped my luggage there. I took a train to Bristol, arrived late and convinced the box office to let me in. Kosmo Vinyl recognized me from L.A. and gave me a photo pass. I stepped on the dark side of the stage, immediately tripped on wires and a rod punctured my leg, and started shooting. I got a ride from a Clash roadie back to his place, was dying to sleep as he told me his life story. I finally made it to hospital three days later to get an antibiotic for my leg infection from that injury (but it didn't slow me down).

The Clash always delivered the most passionate, energetic, throbbing, riveting shows. I love the spontaneous interaction between all of them — something that is very rare in most bands. They felt every word, every note, and we were rewarded with indescribable memories. They were heroes in England — their stages just large enough to move around, but accessible to shoot either from balconies above or occasionally on stage beside them. What a fitting end to my punk photography life! First band, the Ramones in Los Angeles; last band, the Clash in England.

This Clash sequence is thrilling, like the key frames of a storyboard. I remember the stage being flooded with back lights, resulting in this luminous series of shots, my favorite shown here. The band is so united and you can imagine yourself in the audience, fists pumping the air, breathless and exhilarated. I love the expressions from the audience in these shots of Joe Strummer — the pensive, teary-eyed blonde woman at Joe's feet and the lad in the white T-shirt, eyes closed, mouth open. Joe was the most amazing person to photograph: expressively animated, not just in his face but in his whole body. The whole band truly gave their all.

A perfect photo to say goodbye: my dear L.A. pals in an English pub, giving me the thumbs up. Life was changing, video was beginning, the bands that I loved were either touring or breaking up, but new generations of exciting music and entertainment were being developed. But I never gave up my dream that some day people would appreciate what we did, and would love my photos as much as I loved taking them.

This is but a small sample of my archive and stories. I don't know how I did all I did in four years and created this archive of stunning images. I recently looked at thousands of color pictures of the Clash in England and couldn't stop crying, seeing those breathtaking shots, feeling the energy, so vivid after so many years. True art does that: it reaches down and grabs you and never lets go.

I haven't ever seen most of my photos. I pray I live long enough and figure out how to see and share more. I remember so much, and carry this deep within a chamber of my heart. I don't live in the past, but I was blessed to be part of this — the last time we could be American bohemians.

X signed with Slash on the roof of Slash's Beverly Boulevard offices — "We set the trash on fire." Jay Jenkins, X's lawyer and manager, with Billy Zoom, John Doe, D.J. Bonebrake, Exene, Bob Biggs, and the dearly missed Top Jimmy.

Opposite: Ultravox's John Foxx at the Whisky in December, 1979 (that effect was not planned). Ultravox were wonderful.

The Go-Go's played the Starwood in January, 1980. This pose captures their personalities, with Margot's ready smile, Gina's openness, reserved Charlotte, and Jane and Belinda framing the image with their arms crossed.

A rare color shot of the Hong Kong Café in the heart of L.A.'s Chinatown in March, 1980. I love this shot for so many reasons, not least for catching Top Jimmy at the mic with his best pals, X.

Previous pages: Gun Club's Jeffrey Lee Pierce at the Wilton Hilton Valentine's Day Surreal Party, 1980. Tomata du Plenty, Cherie the Penguin, Micol Sinatra (RIP), and Marcie Blaustein.

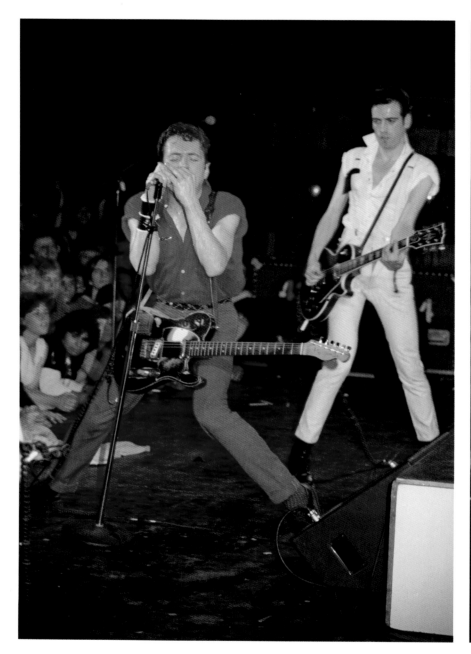

The Clash: Joe Strummer and Mick Jones at the Santa Monica Civic Auditorium, March 3, 1980.

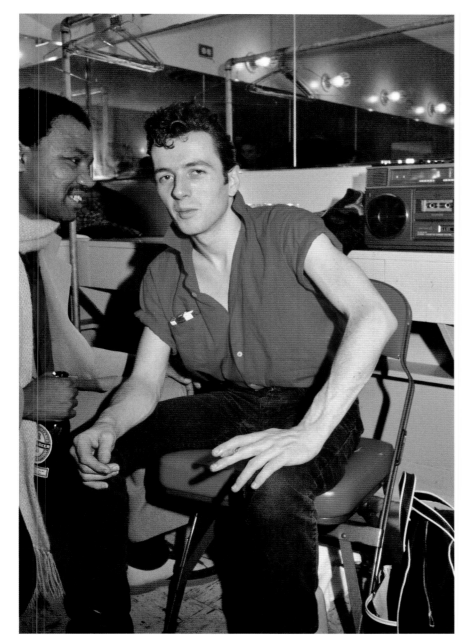

Joe backstage and Paul, the Golden God, onstage.

X during the filming of *Decline of Western Civilization*, at Club 88 in West L.A., in the spring of 1980.

Exene chose this kneeling shot for the cover of the *Live at the Masque* CDs she produced. She so often reminded me of a punk Judy Garland. This rapidly became a defining, iconic image.

Exene and John looking upward, their arms pale against the darkness. John Doe always reminded me of a young, sexy Jim Morrison, especially in these leather pants at the Whisky.

Following pages: The Go-Go's live at the Whisky in March, 1980, and the close friendship between X and the Go-Go's: Billy Zoom, Charlotte, Gina, Jane, original bassist and co-founder Margot, and John Doe.

Masque founder Brendan Mullen with Casey Cola at the Go-Go's goodbye party, March, 1980.

Following pages: Exene wearing her just-buried sister Mireille's Dodgers jacket on stage at the Hollywood Palladium, April, 1980.

John Lydon and a little boy at the PiL show at the Olympic Auditorium, May 4, 1980.

X backstage with producer Ray Manzarek and X's unofficial fifth member, Top Jimmy. April, 1980, and opposite, with director Penelope Spheeris.

Darby Crash, with his new mohawican hairstyle and wearing his new discovery, Adam and the Ants, which surprised his friends and fans.

Exene, Margot, and the Go-Go's manager Ginger Canzoneri at a party in London, England.

Previous pages: The Clash in England, June, 1980.

Darby and Farrah in England, with Jordan in Queen Elizabeth I white face makeup. Darby's hair is not as exaggerated as in the recent Germs film. He's wearing the Germs blue circle armband.

Guitarist Steve Jones (Jonesy) meeting Billy Zoom for the first time.

Drummers Paul Cook (Cookie) and D.J. Bonebrake.

Following page: John's thumbs up, with Exene and Claude "Kick Boy" Bessy (RIP) behind him.